C

Canadian English is the only textbook of its kind to introduce the study of Canadian English in the context of basic concepts of linguistics and socio-linguistics. The book provides foundational information on linguistic prin-ciples and the different branches of sociolinguistics, including the difficulty of distinguishing languages from dialects, the difference between standards and norms, the regional and social conditioning of linguistic variation, the social motivations of language change and the relation between language and social identity. Each chapter discusses methods of collecting and analyzing socio-linguistic data and engages with current issues in sociolinguistics, such as new-dialect formation, language and social identity and ongoing language change. This volume is a dynamic introduction to Canadian English, making it key reading for students in Canadian English, varieties of English, language variation and sociolinguistics.

James A. Walker is Associate Professor in the Department of Languages, Literatures and Linguistics at York University, Canada.

Praise for this book:

"Walker has successfully detailed the historical settlement of Canada and embedded it in the study of contemporary dialects. He discusses a full range of Canadian features from words—such as *chesterfield*—to sounds, morphology, syntax and even the shibboleth *eh*, offering readers a comprehensive understanding of this unique variety."

Sali Tagliamonte, *University of Toronto*

"Anyone teaching an introductory class on Canadian English will appreciate this concise, accessible text. It assumes no background knowledge, but is rich in theoretical, methodological and empirical detail. Walker provides a strong backbone upon which to elaborate content as appropriate, and the mini-projects enable students to engage with data—the best way to learn."

Alexandra D'Arcy, *University of Victoria*

Canadian English

A Sociolinguistic Perspective

James A. Walker

Routledge
Taylor & Francis Group

NEW YORK AND LONDON

First published 2015
by Routledge
711 Third Avenue, New York, NY 10017

and by Routledge
2 Park Square, Milton Park, Abingdon, Oxon, OX14 4RN

Routledge is an imprint of the Taylor & Francis Group, an informa business

© 2015 Taylor & Francis

Library of Congress Cataloging-in-Publication Data
Walker, James A.
    Canadian English : sociolinguistic perspective / James A. Walker,
York University.
        pages cm
    Includes bibliographical references and index.
    1. English language—Canada.   2. Sociolinguistics—Canada.   3. English language—Canada—History.   4. English language—Study and teaching—Canada.   5. Canadianisms.   I. Title.
    PE3208.W35 2015
    427'.971—dc23
    2014047646

ISBN: 978-0-415-53536-6 (hbk)
ISBN: 978-0-415-53537-3 (pbk)
ISBN: 978-0-203-55143-1 (ebk)

Typeset in Minion
by Apex CoVantage, LLC

Contents

Figures

66

Tables

Acknowledgments

The idea for this book stems from a senior-level course on Canadian English from a sociolinguistic perspective that I began teaching a number of years ago. In assembling key readings for the course, I discovered that many of them were not easily accessible (out of print or available only in obscure publications) or were outdated, reflecting a view of English-speaking Canada unfamiliar to students living in an increasingly diverse society. My initial idea was to make these readings more widely available as a reader, but Ivy Ip at Routledge sensibly urged me to write a more integrated volume that would incorporate some discussion of sociolinguistic methodology. The book would serve as a guide or a gateway to further reading, rather than as a comprehensive overview of work on Canadian English, something that Charles Boberg's (2010) excellent monograph already provides. In addition, any book that aims to be comprehensive will quickly become out-of-date because of the ever-growing body of sociolinguistic research on Canadian English.

Apart from the students in courses that I have taught in Canada and Germany, who served as "guinea pigs" in developing the materials that became this book, I owe thanks to a number of people. Leah Babb-Rosenfeld and Elysse Preposi at Routledge have not only been diligent in gently pushing me along, but they have also been understanding and generous with extensions to deadlines. Rena Torres Cacoullos and Judith Nylveh gave the entire manuscript a thorough reading, and Charles Boberg, Sali Tagliamonte and Alexandra D'Arcy provided detailed comments on chapters dealing with their areas of expertise, which greatly improved the book. I thank them for their time, effort and collegiality, though I bear ultimate responsibility for any shortcomings.

A number of personal and professional factors conspired to distract me from completing the book, most prominent being my father's death in 2012, after a long illness. Anthony (Tony) Walker, who had immigrated to Canada from England as a teenager with his parents and younger brother, did his best to modify his Yorkshire accent, but he never quite mastered the vowel system of Canadian English. Perhaps it was growing up with exposure to another variety of English from an early age that led to my interest in linguistic variation generally and to Canadian English in particular.

I dedicate this book to the memory of my father and to all the other immigrants who have helped to make Canada the great country that it is.

1

Introduction

1.1 WHAT IS "CANADIAN ENGLISH"?

At first glance, this question might seem odd. Everyone knows what we're talking about when we say "American English" or "British English" or "Australian English", so why shouldn't there be a "Canadian English"?

Part of the problem with using a term like "Canadian English" (or indeed, a term for any "national" variety of English) is that it implies a higher degree of differentiation from other dialects of English than might actually exist. The English spoken in Canada is mutually intelligible with varieties of English spoken elsewhere in the world; that is, a speaker of Canadian English can be understood by a speaker of Australian English, and vice versa. All dialects of English have a lot in common: where there are differences, they tend to be relatively superficial, such as different words for the same thing or different pronunciations for the same word. We can often identify where someone comes from in the English-speaking world by their choice of words and how they pronounce them. In addition, the term "Canadian English" glosses over the fact that the English spoken across most of Canada is very similar to American English. Most people outside of North America don't even notice the difference.

Another problem with using a term like "Canadian English" to identify a national dialect is that it also implies a higher degree of *internal* consistency than might actually exist. For example, some Canadians and Americans will talk about how much they like "a British accent", ignoring the wide range of regional (as well as social) distinctions among the varieties of English spoken in the British Isles, not only in terms of pronunciation and vocabulary, but also in their grammatical structure—in fact, there may be more variation *within* British English than there is between British English and other national dialects! While the English spoken in Canada does not show the same degree of diversity in pronunciation, vocabulary and grammar as is found in British English, there are audible differences between the English spoken in central and western Canada and that spoken in the Atlantic provinces (especially Newfoundland and Labrador), and even within each of these varieties there is some evidence for fine-grained phonetic distinctions and regional vocabulary.

While acknowledging these problems, I believe that there is some value in retaining the term "Canadian English". First, although the term *dialect* is linguistically questionable and most linguists prefer to use the more neutral term *variety* (see Chapter 3), the notion of "dialect" may be psychologically, politically and/or socially meaningful for the people who speak it. As a result, this meaning can influence not only their beliefs about and attitudes toward language usage and to other speakers, but also their own linguistic behaviour. Finally, since dialect surveys of "American English" usually ignore speakers north of the Canada–US border (although the recent *Phonological Atlas of North American English* [Labov, Ash and Boberg 2006] is a notable exception), the English spoken in Canada has figured only marginally in studies of North American English.

1.2 WHY A SOCIOLINGUISTIC APPROACH?

When most people think of a language (or a dialect), they usually think of something static and self-contained. In fact, most public discourse around language takes this view. For example, you probably have an idea of what "English" is, or what "American English" is, as well as what it isn't. You also probably don't like the way people younger than you speak or the way people from other places speak, and you might even feel that the way they speak is ruining your language. But the reality is that each language includes a great deal of variation (regional and social) and is constantly changing.

In the early 20th century, the Swiss linguist Ferdinand de Saussure made a distinction between looking at a language as it develops over time (**diachronic linguistics**) and trying to understand a language as it exists right now, without reference to its past (**synchronic linguistics**). Saussure's distinction stemmed in part from his desire to move away from 19th-century *philology*, which was concerned with understanding the history and interrelationship of languages, and so necessarily took a diachronic approach to the study of language. In the 20th century, the new discipline of *linguistics* was concerned with studying each language as a self-contained structural system (in Saussure's terms, the object of linguistics should be to study the abstract system *langue*, or "language", rather than what people actually do with that system, *parole*, or "speech"). As a result, **descriptive linguistics** has generally been concerned with writing a *grammar* of each language, which is then taken to represent the linguistic system of that language. (This concern was especially prominent in the United States in the early 20th century, when linguists were hurrying to document the many disappearing indigenous languages of North America.)

In the 1950s and 1960s, the description of individual languages gave way to the study of language in the individual speaker's brain, an approach pioneered by Noam Chomsky in a theoretical framework initially known as transformational-generative grammar (or simply, **generative grammar**) that underwent further refinements as Government and Binding (or Principles and Parameters) in the 1980s and since the mid-1990s as the Minimalist Program. In this theoretical framework, language is seen as a mental faculty that allows the speaker to produce and understand grammatical sentences (i.e. utterances that conform to the linguistic system), and it is the object of linguistic inquiry to figure out the nature of that mental faculty, rather than the production and understanding of speech or the grammar of particular languages. This approach has come to dominate linguistics, at least in North America.

At the same time that generative grammar was being developed in the 1960s, some people who studied language became dissatisfied with the increasing exclusion from linguistic analysis of the social and cultural aspects of language. Some began to examine the link between language and culture from an anthropological perspective (**linguistic anthropology**, or anthropological linguistics, also referred to as the **ethnography of speaking**), with some examining large-scale patterns of language use across communities, such as why people speak a particular language, when they speak it and with whom (**sociology of language**), and others studying the quantitative patterning of linguistic behaviour across different social groups and situations (**sociolinguistic variation and change**). While the approaches and methods of these different schools of linguistics all differ, they are generally subsumed under the heading of *sociolinguistics*, since they are all concerned not only with the structural aspects of language, but also with the role that language plays in the social and cultural life of human beings.

A purely linguistic approach to Canadian English would simply describe the structural aspects of the dialects of English spoken in Canada: pronunciation, vocabulary and grammar. However, this description would leave unexplored and unexplained a great deal of information that is relevant for understanding why English is spoken in Canada, why it has the form it does and how its speakers view and use it. For these reasons, in this book I have decided to take a sociolinguistic approach to the study of Canadian English, being concerned not only with its structural (or *language-internal*) aspects but also with the social, cultural and ideological (or *language-external*) aspects of the varieties of English spoken in Canada.

1.3 STRUCTURE OF THE BOOK

This book is intended not only as an introduction to and overview of Canadian English, but also as an introduction to the methods used in sociolinguistic approaches to the study of language. Rather than providing a comprehensive overview of the ever-expanding literature on the study of English in Canada (see Boberg 2010), I have tried to present the key facts about Canadian English and a representative sample of key and recent works to illustrate these facts. The book is divided into chapters that deal with different aspects of the study of Canadian English, each of which includes discussion of the methodology relevant to its topic.

Chapter 2, "Some Basics", provides a general overview of the study of language and the discipline of sociolinguistics and introduces the reader to different methodological approaches to studying language, with a particular focus on sociolinguistic variation and change, the main methodological approach adopted in this book. Readers who already have some background in linguistics, and specifically in sociolinguistics, may wish to skip this chapter. "What is Linguistics?" outlines the different areas of study in linguistics: phonetics (the study of speech production), phonology (the study of sound systems), morphology (the study of word structure), syntax (the study of word order) and semantics (the study of meaning). "What is Sociolinguistics?" outlines the major approaches to the study of language in its social context: sociology of language (macro sociolinguistics), the ethnography of speaking or linguistic anthropology (qualitative sociolinguistics) and language variation and change (quantitative sociolinguistics).

Chapter 3, "The Origins and Development of Canadian English", examines the factors involved in the formation of new dialects and the historical and demographic developments that led to the development of the English language in Canada. "The Origins and Spread of English Dialects" takes a large-scale view of the relationships among the different dialects of English spoken around the world. "Principles of New Dialect Formation" looks at different theories of how new dialects come about, why they are similar to each other and why they differ. "The History of Canadian English" presents an overview of the major historical events in the development of English in Canada, preceding the American Revolution through the War of 1812 and Confederation, to the demographic shifts that took place in the 20th century. "Canadian English as a New Dialect" applies the principles of new-dialect formation to the development and features of Canadian English.

The remaining chapters of the book outline variation in the structural features of Canadian English and how they differ from other varieties of English and regionally within Canada. Chapter 4, "Lexical Variation", focuses on the lexical features of Canadian English, not only differences between the vocabulary of

Canadian English and that of other varieties of English, but also regional variation within Canadian English. This chapter also provides an overview of the methods of dialect topography in studying regional variation in vocabulary and examines the extent to which words can be considered "Canadianisms", as well as discussing dictionaries of Canadian English and regional dictionaries. Chapter 5, "Phonetic and Phonological Variation", focuses on the sound systems of Canadian English, not only the units of the phonological system but also their phonetic realizations. Chapter 6, "Grammatical Variation", focuses on the grammatical and discourse features of Canadian English. Chapter 7, "The Present and the Future of Canadian English", considers ongoing changes in Canadian English, using the apparent-time construct and age-based distributions, as well as the sociolinguistic consequences of increasing ethnolinguistic diversity in English Canada's largest cities, and ends with some consideration of the long-term effects that these changes might have on the character of Canadian English.

2

Some Basics

2.0 INTRODUCTION

Linguistics and sociolinguistics are like other specialized disciplines in that they use terms and methods that are particular to them. In the rest of the book, I assume that readers have a basic understanding of these terms and methods. Those readers who do may skip forward to the next chapter. This chapter is intended to provide readers with a basic understanding of linguistics and sociolinguistics. In the first part, I discuss linguistics and its various branches. In the second part, I discuss different approaches to the study of language in its social context.

2.1 WHAT IS LINGUISTICS?

Linguistics is a scholarly discipline that is concerned with the study of language. When I tell people that I'm a linguist, the two most common questions they ask me right away are "How many languages do you speak?" and "What language do you teach?" These questions undoubtedly stem from the colloquial meaning of the word *linguist*, which usually means "someone who speaks a lot of languages". While some linguists do tend to focus on some aspects of a particular language (e.g. the sound pattern of English), linguistics is not concerned with studying an individual language but rather with the study of language in general: what its structure is, where it comes from and what it is used for. Because language is so intimately caught up with every aspect of human life, it can be studied from a number of different perspectives:

- *Physical*: How is language stored in the human brain? How does it get there? What is the nature of mental representation? How are other activities of

the brain (knowledge, thoughts, feelings) converted into language, and how is language physically produced as speech?
- *Structural*: What units does language consist of? What governs how those units are combined or altered?
- *Cultural/social*: What do people use language for? What role does it play in expressing and influencing human culture? What role does it play in creating and expressing social meaning? What effect does it have on society and culture?

Thanks to this breadth of potential perspectives under which language can be studied, linguistics is variously considered to be a cognitive science, a social science and part of the humanities.

Within linguistics, we normally distinguish **core linguistics** from those approaches to the study of language that overlap with other scholarly disciplines, such as psychology (**psycholinguistics**) and sociology (**sociolinguistics**). Core linguistics is concerned with questions that are relevant only to the study of language structure:

How are sounds produced and used (**phonetics** and **phonology**)?
How are sounds put together into words (**morphology**)?
How are words put together into sentences (**syntax**)?
How is meaning expressed linguistically (**semantics**)?

In the following sections, I will provide a brief overview of each of these areas.

2.1.1 Phonetics: The Study of Speech Production

Phonetics is the area of linguistics that concerns how speech sounds are produced by the human vocal apparatus. One goal of phonetics is the characterization of *any and all* possible human speech sounds. To further this goal, the International Phonetic Association has developed a set of symbols (the International Phonetic Alphabet, or IPA; see Appendix 1), each of which represents a sound that exists in at least one of the world's languages. As phonetics is suitable to the study of all languages (at least, all *spoken* languages; signed languages share certain properties of spoken languages but are obviously distinguished by the physical means of their expression), phonetic analysis does not need to refer to (or even to know anything about!) the language in which speech is produced.

There are two ways of doing phonetic analysis, each of which is characterized by different methodologies (though in practice one does not exclude the other): **articulatory phonetics** and **acoustic phonetics**.

Articulatory Phonetics

Articulatory phonetics is concerned with describing the physiological arrangement of the human organs involved in the production of sound, the **vocal tract:**

- Lungs
- Vocal cords
- Mouth (or oral cavity)
- Nasal passage (or nasal cavity)
- Tongue
- Lips (see Figure 2.1)

The articulatory property of a speech sound may be described in words (e.g. "voiceless alveolar stop"), but it is more convenient to describe it by using a phonetic symbol, indicated by enclosing it within brackets (e.g. [t]).

The production of speech sounds begins with the lungs, which create airflow by expelling air (**egressive**) (though sometimes by drawing it in [**ingressive**]). Other parts of the vocal tract act in different ways to produce changes to the airflow that can be used to distinguish speech sounds. The most basic type of change to the airflow, **phonation**, involves changing the state of the vocal cords. The vocal cords can be held close together so that they vibrate as air passes through them, setting up a series of resonating bursts of energy,

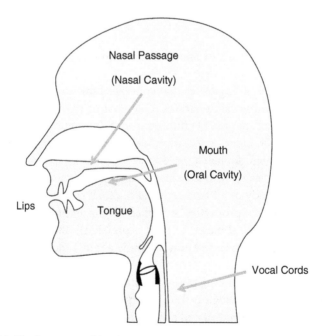

FIGURE 2.1 The human vocal tract

resulting in a **voiced** sound. If the vocal cords are held far apart, they do not vibrate, and the sound produced is **voiceless**. Other phonation types involve holding the vocal cords together or apart to different degrees (a "creaky" voice) or tightening them to produce a higher pitch (falsetto).

The airflow can be further modified as it passes through the mouth or nose. The main division between speech sounds is **vowels** and **consonants**. Producing a vowel involves changing the shape of the airflow by configuring the tongue at different positions within the mouth. Placing the tip of the tongue toward the roof of the mouth produces a **high** vowel like [i] in *reed* or [u] in *rued*, while bunching the tongue at the bottom of the mouth produces a **low** vowel like [ɑ] in *rod*. Mid vowels, like [e] in *made* and [o] in *mode*, are produced at positions between high and low vowels. Vowel height may be further distinguished as **tense**, like [i] in *heed*, or **lax**, like [ɪ] in *hid* (although this distinction is often specific to individual languages such as English rather than universal). Positioning the tongue toward the teeth produces **front** vowels such as [i] and [e], while pulling the tongue toward the throat produces **back** vowels such as [u] and [o]. Vowels produced in the middle of the mouth, such as [ʌ] in *cut*, or the unstressed vowel schwa [ə], are called **central**. Another dimension that distinguishes vowels is whether the lips are pursed or spread. Pursing the lips produces **rounded** vowels such as [o] and [u], while spreading the lips produces unrounded vowels such as [i] and [e]. Vowels can be combined into **diphthongs**, which consist of multiple vowels pronounced sequentially (though one vowel usually has more prominence), such as [aw] in *cow* and [ay] in *why*. Thus, an articulatory description of any vowel involves stating its height, frontness/backness and rounding. For example, [u] may be described as a "high back rounded vowel". Vowels can also be distinguished in terms of **length** (e.g. short [a] vs. long [a:]), as in German *Stadt* [ʃtat] ("city") versus *Staat* [ʃtaːt] ("state"), and may be **nasalized** by opening the nasal passage: [ã], as in Portuguese *pão* [pãw] ("bread"). Table 2.1 provides a chart with some of the cross-linguistically most common vowels and their positions in the mouth.

TABLE 2.1

Some Common Vowels

		Front		Central	Back	
		Rounded	*Unrounded*		*Rounded*	*Unrounded*
High	(Tense)	y	i		u	ɯ
	(Lax)		ɪ		ʊ	
Mid	(Tense)	ø	e	ə	o	ɤ
	(Lax)		ɛ	ʌ	ɔ	
Low			æ	a	ɑ	ɒ

Producing a consonant involves constricting the airflow by placing a moving articulator (the tongue or the lips) at a stationary place of articulation. The degree of constriction is referred to as the **manner of articulation**: completely blocking the airflow produces a **stop** (or **plosive**), such as [p] or [t], while partial constriction ranges from a more closed sound referred to as a **fricative**, such as [f] (or more "hissy" sibilants, such as [s]) to a more vowel-like **glide** (or **approximant**), such as [w] or [j]. Different degrees of constriction can occur in a single sound, such as an affricate, which begins with complete constriction and ends with partial constriction (think of the final sound of *catch* [tʃ], which combines the final sounds of *cat* [t] and *cash* [ʃ]). Most consonants are produced in the mouth, but if the passage at the back of the throat is opened, the airflow passes through the nasal cavity instead and a **nasal** consonant is produced. For example, in producing the consonant [m], the lips completely block airflow through the mouth and airflow passes instead through the nose. Consonants may be voiced or voiceless. For example, the difference between [t] and [d] is that the first sound is voiceless and the second is voiced. Consonants that are always voiced—that is, those that (normally) have no voiceless counterpart, such as [r] and [l]—are referred to as **sonorant**.

The **place of articulation** refers to the point in the vocal tract where the airstream is closed. If the lips are closed, then **labial** consonants are produced, such as [p] or [m]. If the incisor teeth are placed against the lower lip, a **labiodental** consonant is produced, such as [f]. Placing the tip of the tongue against the ridge behind the incisors (the alveolum) produces **alveolar** consonants, such as [t] or [s], while those produced further back along the hard palate are **palatal** (we don't have such sounds in English but a palatal fricative is represented by *x* in Mandarin Chinese, as in the name of the ancient city *Xi'an*), or **palato-alveolar,** such as [tʃ] or [ʃ], as in the final consonants of *catch* and *cash*. Consonants produced by placing the back of the tongue even further back against the soft palate (the velum) are **velar**, such as [k] or [ŋ]. Consonants produced by constricting the vocal cords, such as [h], are **glottal**. In addition to their primary place of articulations, consonants may have **secondary articulation**. For example, English speakers pronounce the voiceless stops [p], [t] and [k] at the beginning of a word with **aspiration** (a small puff of air after the release). The first sound of the words *pin, tin* and *kin* are the aspirated stops [pʰ], [tʰ] and [kʰ], respectively. An articulatory description of any consonant involves stating its voicing and place and manner of articulation (and secondary articulation, if relevant). For example, [tʰ] would be described as a voiceless aspirated alveolar stop, because there is complete constriction of the airflow (manner) at the alveolar ridge (place), the vocal cords are not vibrating (voicing) and there is a puff of air produced after release (secondary articulation).

Consonants and vowels (**segments**) are grouped together into syllables to constitute the basic components of speech, but other aspects of the speech signal may enter into the production of speech sounds to convey more subtle distinctions (**suprasegmentals**). **Stress** has to do with the relative strength with which each syllable within a word is pronounced. For example, the difference between the noun *permit* and the verb *permit* is that the first syllable is stressed (more prominent) in the first word, whereas the second syllable is stressed in the second word. **Intonation** is the pitch or tune of the speech signal. Some languages, like Chinese, use pitch to create distinctions in tone between words, but in English pitch is used primarily to distinguish statements from questions. For example, compare the intonation of *"You're coming with us to the party"* and *"You're coming with us to the party?"*.

Acoustic Phonetics

Because articulatory phonetics relies on human hearing, it has been criticized as impressionistic, imprecise and subject to the auditory limitations of the (individual) human ear. As a result, phonetic analysis has come to rely more and more not only on human perception, but also on more precise recording technology and computer software, allowing a more objective method for characterizing speech sounds. For the most part, this technology relies on the manifestation of the various articulatory configurations discussed in the preceding section as a physical **sound wave**: the vibration of the vocal cords creates alternating bursts of compressed and rarefied air featuring different amounts of energy, which are modified by the articulators as they leave the mouth, travel through the intervening air and (ideally) arrive at the ear of a hearer, where the sound waves are then interpreted as speech sounds by the hearer's brain. Acoustic phonetics is concerned with the physical properties of the sound wave.

Modern acoustic software allows us easily to produce a visual display of the sound wave. In the following discussion I make use of the computer program Praat (Boersma and Weenink 2015). The upper half of Figure 2.2

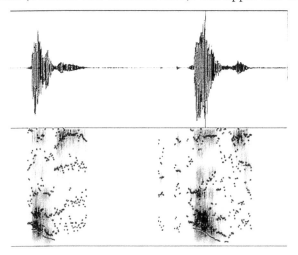

FIGURE 2.2 Sound wave and spectrogram of the author saying *house* (noun) and *house* (verb)

displays the **waveform** of me saying *house* (as a noun) and then *house* (as a verb)—the *x*-axis represents time and the *y*-axis shows the amplitude, or the amount of change in air pressure. Note that the amplitude of the wave is greatest when I am producing the vowel (in this case, a diphthong [ɑw] or [əw]) and weakest when I am producing consonants (especially the voiceless glottal fricative [h]).

Waveforms are useful for distinguishing broad classes of sounds—vowels versus consonants, fricatives versus stops, voiced versus voiceless sounds—but they leave out a lot of detail about the place of articulation. We can see where the vowels in Figure 2.2 are, but how do we know *which* vowels they are? A **spectrogram** provides a visual display not only of the sound wave, but also where the resonant frequencies of that sound wave occur, as measured in Hertz (Hz). The lower part of Figure 2.2 shows a spectrogram of the same sound wave. The darker shadings show the concentrations of energy, which represent the resonant frequencies in the sound wave. The program used to display the spectrogram (Praat) also displays the peaks of energy, or formants, associated with the vowel sound. The lowest line is a measurement of **fundamental frequency** (F_0), which tells us something about the pitch. Each of the dotted lines above the fundamental frequency represents a different vowel **formant**: the first formant (F_1), the second formant (F_2), the third formant (F_3) and so on. Normally we use the first two (and sometimes the third) formants as indications of vowel position: F_1 corresponds to vowel

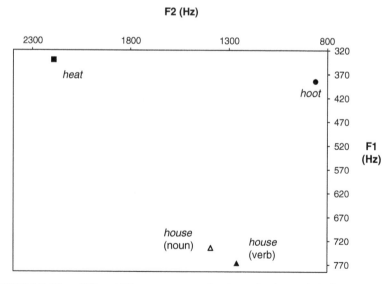

FIGURE 2.3 Plot of F2 and F1 measurements for the author's vowels in *heat, hoot, house* (noun) and *house* (verb)

height and F_2 corresponds to vowel frontness/backness, with higher values indicating greater lowness and frontness, respectively. If we pick a point along the formant (normally where the vowel is least affected by the preceding or following sound) and measure the formant values, we can plot F_1 and F_2 to show the position of the vowel as it would appear in a vowel chart. Figure 2.3 plots the F_1/F_2 positions of my vowels in *house* (noun) and *house* (verb) from the spectrogram in Figure 2.2, as well as the positions of my vowels [i] in *heat* and [u] in *hoot*, for comparison (note that to make the vowel positions resemble those normally used in vowel charts we have to reverse the direction of the numbers in each axis). You can see that my pronunciation of [ɑw] differs depending on the voicing of the following consonant (see Chapter 5 to find out why!). Acoustic phonetics can be used for a number of purposes, but its most common application in sociolinguistic research is the measurement of vowels.

2.1.2 Phonology

In contrast to phonetics, which is concerned with the physical production of sound and is not specific to any language, phonology concerns the way that sounds are organized within a particular language. Since Saussure, the fundamental unit of sound patterns has been taken to be the **phoneme**, which serves a contrastive function within each language to distinguish between words with different meanings. For example, the voicing of consonants in English is phonemic because it distinguishes between pairs of words that differ only in the voicing of a single sound, such as *pat* and *bat*. Thus, we can say that English has the phonemes /p/ and /b/, indicated by putting the phonetic symbol between forward slashes. Note that voicing is not phonemic in all languages: in Chinese, [toŋ] and [doŋ] do not mean different things. However, [toŋ] and [tʰoŋ], which are differentiated by aspiration, are contrastive in Chinese (one means "pain", the other means "hunger"), whereas in English aspiration is not contrastive. Table 2.2 provides a phonemic inventory for the consonants of English.

Differences in pronunciation that are phonemic serve to signal contrasts in meaning, but some phonetic differences are not meaningful; rather, they depend on the position or surrounding context in which the sound occurs. For example, although in German, as in English, voicing is phonemic, differences in voicing are neutralized at the end of a word, so *bund* ("union") and *bunt* ("ribbon") are pronounced the same [bunt]. These **allophones**, or predictably different phonetic realizations of the same phoneme, are said to be in **complementary distribution**: the environments in which each realization of the phoneme occurs do not overlap with each other. So we would not expect to find a [d] at the end of a word in German.

One way to think about the relationship between allophones is that they result from the operation of phonological processes on a basic or underlying form of the

TABLE 2.2

Phonemic Inventory of Consonants in English

		BILABIAL	LABIO-DENTAL	INTER-DENTAL	ALVEO-LAR	PALATO-ALVEOLAR	PALATAL	VELAR	GLOTTAL
Stop	Voiceless	p			t			k	
	Voiced	b			d			g	
Fricative	Voiceless		f	θ	s	ʃ			h
	Voiced		v	ð	z	ʒ			
Affricate	Voiceless					tʃ			
	Voiced					dʒ			
Approximant		(w)			r		j	(w)	
Nasal		m			n			ŋ	
Lateral					l				

phoneme. If we take the allophone with the least restricted occurrence to represent the underlying form, we can view the allophonic differences as

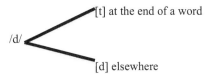

/d/ — [t] at the end of a word
/d/ — [d] elsewhere

In this approach, there is an underlying form of the phoneme /d/ that changes its voicing depending on the context in which it occurs. We could also express this as a devoicing rule (2.1) that takes the phonemic input (/d/) and produces a phonetic output ([t]) in the appropriate context. Using a system of shorthand notation developed by Noam Chomsky and Morris Halle (1968), we could express the rule as in (2.2) (where/means "in the context of", __ indicates the position of the sound undergoing the rule and # represents the end of a word).

(2.1)   DEVOICING RULE: A /d/ becomes [t] at the end of a word.
(2.2)   /d/ → [t] / __ #

Note that we do not need to provide a second rule to account for the allophone [d]: where the rule does not apply, /d/ retains its voicing. Apart from rules of devoicing or voicing, we find phonological rules that alter aspects of manner (e.g. a stop becomes a fricative in some environment) or place (e.g. a velar becomes a palatal or an alveolar becomes palatalized in some environment). There are also phonological rules that involve an entire segment, deleting or inserting sounds in particular contexts.

Normally, phonological processes or rules do not target one phoneme in particular but act on a set of phonemes that have something in common. For example, German devoicing occurs not just with /d/, but also /b/ and /g/, as formulated in (2.3). But since all three sounds have something in common (they are all voiced stops), it seems redundant to write three separate rules. If we tweak the notation, with { } indicating "or", we can combine the rules in (2.3) into one rule (2.4).

(2.3)   /b/ → [p] / __ #
         /d/ → [t] / __ #
         /g/ → [k] / __ #

(2.4) $\begin{Bmatrix} /b/ \\ /d/ \\ /g/ \end{Bmatrix} \rightarrow \begin{Bmatrix} [p] \\ [t] \\ [k] \end{Bmatrix} / \_\_ \#$

A more elegant way of simplifying the formulation of phonological processes or rules is to recognize that sounds form "natural" classes that share phonological characteristics. Rather than formulating rules in terms of phonemes, we can break phonemes down to their constituent characteristics. In phonological theory these characteristics are most commonly expressed as **distinctive features**, where each phoneme or allophone is characterized by the presence or absence of a feature value. For example, we can propose a feature [voiced] and characterize voiced sounds as [+voiced] and voiceless sounds as [-voiced]. Similarly, we can distinguish between sounds in which the airflow is stopped [-continuant], from those in which the airflow is unimpeded [+continuant]. This characterization of phonemes in terms of their features allows us to reformulate rules to target classes of sounds based on the shared features. Thus, we can reformulate the rule of German word-final devoicing as:

(2.5)   DEVOICING RULE: A voiced stop becomes voiceless at the end of a word.

$$\begin{bmatrix} -\text{continuant} \\ +\text{voiced} \end{bmatrix} \rightarrow [-\text{voiced}] \ / \ \_\_ \ \#$$

Varieties of the same language may share the same phonological system but differ in the phonetic realization of phonemes. For example, all English dialects have the diphthong phoneme /ay/, but the phonetic value of that diphthong is different depending on where you come from. While listeners may pick up on these differences as an "accent", they are for the most part able to map the phonetic realization to the correct phoneme.

2.1.3 Morphology

Phonology allows speakers of a language to make distinctions between sounds, but in order for language to function as a system for conveying meaning, there must be a link between sound and meaning. Note that this link is completely *arbitrary*, something pointed out by Ferdinand de Saussure at the beginning of the 20th century; that is, there is no reason why, for example, the string of sounds [kʰæt] should necessarily mean "four-legged furry household pet that meows". In fact, the string of sounds used to refer to this animal differs across languages (e.g. /ʃɑ/ in French and /mɑw/ in Chinese). So how do we understand what any string of sounds means? As the speaker of a language, one of our tasks is to memorize the link between a particular string of sounds and a particular meaning (in Saussure's terms, the link may be arbitrary but it is *conventional*—speakers of a language have a [tacit] agreement that the link exists).

Most people, if asked, would say that the link between sound and meaning is provided by the **word**, but a word is not the smallest unit of language that conveys meaning. For example, *cats* is one word, but it consists of two parts: the string of sounds /kæt/ (the **root** or **stem**), which is linked to the basic meaning of the word (see above), and the sound /s/, which indicates that the speaker is referring to more than one cat. Each of these word parts is a **morpheme**, the smallest unit of language that links form (sound) and meaning. Note that because a word can consist of a single morpheme (a simple or **monomorphemic** word) or multiple morphemes (a complex word), a word may be a morpheme, but a morpheme isn't necessarily a word.

Just as a phoneme may have different phonetic realizations (allophones) depending on the surrounding context, a morpheme may have different phonological realizations (**allomorphs**). Some allomorphs are predictable on the basis of the phonological context. For example, the form of the plural /s/ morpheme in English depends on the nature of the final sound in the stem: voiceless [s] if the preceding sound is voiceless (e.g. *cats*), a syllabic form [əz] if the preceding sound is a sibilant (e.g. *houses*) and [z] everywhere else (e.g. *dogs*, *crows*). For this phonologically conditioned allomorphy (sometimes called *apparent allomorphy*), we could establish a distributional statement or a rule similar to that for the phonological processes discussed in the previous section. In fact, we would probably want to account for this allomorphy through phonological rather than morphological rules.

However, some allomorphs are not predictable from the context. For example, the plural form *-ren* occurs only in the plural *children*, and some nouns have the same form in singular and plural (e.g. *sheep*). In such cases, it does not make sense to propose a rule. Allomorphs that are unpredictable or irregular (*true allomorphy*) simply have to be memorized by the speaker when learning the language. Unlike apparent allomorphy, which can be accounted for through phonology, true allomorphy is clearly part of the morphological system.

The most common ways of building up words out of morphemes are affixation, stem-change and compounding, all of which are found in English. **Affixation** adds a morpheme to the beginning (prefixation) or end (suffixation) of a stem. For example, the verb (stem) *believe* can be changed to an adjective by adding *-able*, a suffix meaning "capable of being VERB-ed", creating the word *believable*. The adjective *believable* (a stem) can be negated by adding *un-*, a prefix meaning "not ADJECTIVE", to create the word *unbelievable*.

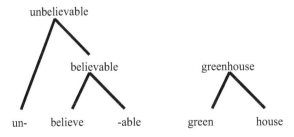

Compounding is similar to affixation, in that morphemes are added to morphemes, but here, rather than adding affixes to a stem, two or more stems are added together. For example, in English the adjective *green* and the noun *house* can be combined to form *greenhouse*, which does not mean "a house that is green", but rather "a house for growing plants". **Stem change** involves modifying the phonological form of the stem rather than adding a morpheme. For example, most verbs in English indicate past tense by suffixing -ed: *walk ~ walked*. However, a verb like *sing* indicates past tense by changing the stem vowel: *sing ~ sang*. English also allows new words to be formed without any changes to the stem (**conversion**, or zero derivation): *run* (verb) ~ *run* (noun).

Morphology is usually divided into two types: derivational and inflectional. **Derivational** morphology changes the basic meaning of the word and/or its grammatical category. **Inflectional** morphology does not change the basic meaning of the word or its grammatical category, but it does add grammatical information. For nouns, it adds information such as number (e.g. plural). For verbs, it adds information such as agreement with the subject (person, number) or information about the tense (past) or aspect (progressive).

2.1.4 Syntax

When most people talk about language, they tend to talk about words, but a language is no more just a list of words than a house is just a pile of bricks. When you speak a language, you do not simply string words together at random to express meaning. Rather, words combine together in complex ways, organized into different levels, such as phrases and sentences. The study of the way that words are put together to form sentences is called *syntax*. Fundamental to syntax is the assumption that words cannot be put together in any order but rather are grouped together into **constituents** that cohere with each other and are differentiated from other parts of the sentence.

The broadest syntactic division we can make in any sentence is between the **subject** (the topic of the idea expressed by the sentence) and the **predicate** (what is being said about the subject). For example, in the sentence *Hecubus walked to school*, the subject is *Hecubus* (*Who* walked to school?) and the predicate is *walked to school* (*What* did Hecubus do?). In English, the predicate is always a verb; if the predicate is anything other than a verb (such as a noun or an adjective), we have to link the subject and predicate with the verb *be*: *Hecubus (is) a cat, Hecubus (is) tall*.

Just as we can divide words into smaller meaningful units, we can divide sentences, subjects and predicates into smaller structural units called **phrases**. Phrases themselves consist of words that can be sorted into different syntactic types or **categories**. **Lexical** categories refer to things in the world outside of language: Nouns (N) refer to things, people or concepts; Verbs (V) refer to activities or states; Adjectives (Adj) and Adverbs (Adv) refer to properties of the other two categories. **Functional** categories express grammatical qualities of or relations between lexical categories. For example, Determiners (Det) like *the* and *a* say something about the definiteness of Nouns (whether the existence of the Noun's referent is already established). Auxiliary (Aux) and modal (Mod) verbs, such as *be, have* and *can*, add information about tense and mood to Verbs. Prepositions (P) such as *to, on* and *with* locate the referents of Nouns with respect to Verbs or to other Nouns.

The overall property of a phrase depends on the syntactic category of its **head**, the word that the phrase is built up from, while other words in the phrase serve to modify or complement the head. A Noun Phrase (NP) such as *the white house* consists of a N (*house*) plus its modifiers, Det (*the*) and Adj (*white*), whereas a Verb Phrase (VP) such as *quickly ate the tofu* consists of a Verb (*ate*) plus (optionally) modifiers, Adv (*quickly*), and (optionally) objects (NP, *the tofu*). A Prepositional Phrase (PP) such as *into the woods* consists of a P (*into*) plus its NP object (*the woods*). As in morphology, the relations between categories within the phrase can be represented using hierarchical tree structures (where S stands for sentence):

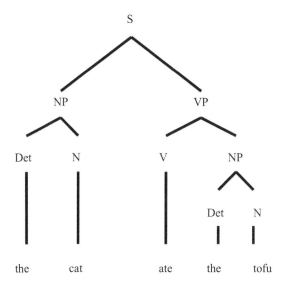

Most theories of syntax assume that hierarchical structures are constrained by **phrase-structure rules** that determine the possible ordering of categories in each language. For example, a language like English has a phrase-structure rule for NPs specifying that Adj precedes N, whereas in Spanish the NP phrase-structure rule would specify that Adj follows N:

(2.6) a. English NP → Det Adj N   *the white house*
       b. Spanish NP → Det N Adj   *la casa blanca*

Apart from phrase structure, syntax exhibits properties of displacement or movement, in that in some sentences constituents occur in different positions. For example, if we want to ask about the object of a verb in English, we replace the object with *what*, although the word does not occur where an object would normally occur, after the verb, but at the beginning of the sentence:

(2.7)   a. *Hecubus is eating tofu*
        b. *What is Hecubus eating ___ ?*

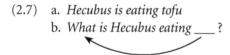

This movement occurs regardless of which part of the sentence we are asking about: *what, who(m), where, why*. Notice that forming a question requires not only moving the *wh*-word to the front of the sentence, but also moving the auxiliary verb *is* before the subject:

(2.8)   *What is Hecubus ___ eating ___ ?*

Auxiliary-verb movement is also used to form a question asking about the verb:

(2.9)   Is Hecubus ___ eating?

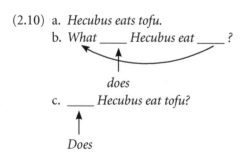

If we think of these movement requirements as rules, then English can be said to have an "auxiliary-movement" rule to form questions and (if there is a *wh*-word involved) a "*wh*-movement" rule.

Other types of syntactic rules involve inserting or deleting constituents. In English, if we form a question in a sentence that does not contain an auxiliary verb, we have to fill the auxiliary position by inserting the "dummy" auxiliary verb *do*:

(2.10) a. *Hecubus eats tofu.*
        b. *What ____ Hecubus eat ____ ?*

             does

        c. ____ *Hecubus eat tofu?*

          Does

Note that the rule of "*do*-insertion" (more commonly referred to as "*do*-support") applies not only in questions but also in any situation where an auxiliary is required. For example, if we make a sentence negative by adding the negator *not*, it must be preceded by an auxiliary:

(2.11) *Hecubus <u>is</u> not eating tofu.*

If there is no auxiliary in the sentence, then *do*-insertion fills the auxiliary position:

(2.12) *Hecubus _____ not eat tofu.*
                     ↑
                 does

Often when we repeat something or we make a comparison, we delete some part of it to avoid sounding repetitious. A rule of ellipsis allows us to do this, though again, if there is no auxiliary in the sentence, *do*-insertion is required:

(2.13) a. *Hecubus is eating tofu and James is ~~eating tofu~~ too.*
        b. *Hecubus eats tofu and James _____ ~~eats tofu~~ too.*
                                          ↑
                                      does

The simplest sentence consists of a single clause, but more complex sentences can be built up by joining clauses together. **Coordination** joins clauses together by using a conjunction such as *and* and *or* (2.14).

(2.14) *Hecubus ate tofu <u>and</u> James ate rice.*

Subordination joins clauses together by making one clause the object of a constituent in another clause. If that constituent is a verb, its clausal object is a **subordinate clause**. If the subordinate clause is declarative, it is (optionally) introduced with the **complementizer** *that*, whereas an interrogative clause is introduced with *if* or *whether*:

(2.15) a. *I know* ⌐
                    └→ **(that)** *Hecubus ate the tofu.*

        b. *I wonder* ⌐
                      └→ **if/whether** *Hecubus ate the tofu.*

A clause that is the object of a noun is a relative clause (restrictive vs. non-restrictive). Relative clauses are introduced by *that* (optional if it indicates the object of the verb) or by a relative *wh*-pronoun, such as *who(m)*, or *which*:

(2.16) *The cat* ⌐   ⌐→ *ate the tofu.*
              └→ ***that/who/which*** *is outside* ─┘

The above examples all involve clauses that contain a verb that is morphologically marked for tense (finite). However, in some cases a verb takes as its object a clause that is infinitival (i.e. it contains a verb that is not marked for tense):

(2.17) *James wants* ⌐
              └→ *Hecubus to eat the tofu.*

If the subjects of both clauses are the same, we can apply a rule of ellipsis:

(2.18) *Hecubus wants* ⌐
              └→ ~~*Hecubus*~~ *to eat the tofu.*

The above examples all involve declarative subordinate clauses. If the clause is a question, the complementizer is *whether* (or *if*):

(2.19) *I wonder* ⌐
              └→ *whether/if Hecubus will eat tofu.*

2.1.5 Semantics

The main purpose of language is communication between human beings, and semantics is the branch of linguistics that examines the question of how meaning is conveyed through language. One of the fundamental principles of semantics is that meaning is *compositional*; that is, the meaning of an expression (a word, a phrase, a sentence) is built up from the meaning of its parts (morpheme, words, phrases). We can study meaning at the level of the word (**lexical semantics**) or at the level of the sentence (**propositional semantics**).

Lexical semantics considers the types of relations that hold between words, such as whether words share meaning (synonymy) or have opposing meanings (antonymy) and whether words can be sorted into classes that share particular properties of meaning. For example, a major division in the meaning of nouns is whether their referents consist of discrete entities that can be counted (e.g. *cats*) or whether they refer to a mass entity (e.g. *water*). Verbs can be divided according to whether they refer to states (*be, have*) or events (*walk, eat*), and events can be further divided into whether they continue (continuous or durative), such as *live*, or are instantaneous (punctual), such as *clap*, as well as whether they have an inherent end point (telic), such as *break*. As we saw in the discussion of morphology above, the principle of compositionality means that the meaning of words can be interpreted from the sum of all the word's component morphemes.

Propositional semantics considers how the different constituents of a sentence combine to convey meaning. As noted above, a sentence can be divided into a subject and a predicate, with a predicate consisting of a verb and its NP arguments, but this syntactic structure does not always correspond with the semantic structure of a sentence. Instead, we can think of the different NPs within the sentence as fulfilling certain semantic (or **thematic**) roles required by the verb, such as the agent (the doer of the action), or the theme (the one to whom the action is done). Consider a pair of sentences that refer to the same event but that have different syntactic configurations, as shown in (2.20): *Hecubus ate the tofu* and *The tofu was eaten by Hecubus*.

(2.20) a. Syntax: Subject   Predicate   Direct Object
                          [*Hecubus* $_{NP}$] [*ate*   [*the tofu* $_{NP}$] $_{VP}$]
         Semantics: Agent   Theme
       b. Syntax: Subject   Predicate
                          [*The tofu* $_{NP}$] [*was eaten* [*by Hecubus* $_{PP}$] $_{VP}$]
         Semantics: Theme   Agent

Propositional semantics also concerns the way in which the event structure of the sentence is conveyed not only through the properties of the verb, but also through the combination of verbs with syntactic arguments and modifiers. In English, all sentences need to be marked for tense, which indicates the relation of the event to the time of speaking. Auxiliary verbs such as *do, be* and *have* serve to carry the marking of tense (as well as agreement with the subject of the verb). The auxiliary verbs *have* and *be* are also implicated in conveying aspect, or the internal composition of events, through their combination with different verbal forms to convey progressive (*he is going*) and perfect (*she had eaten*) tense. Modal verbs such as *can, may* and *must* add further meaning to the sentence by indicating the speaker's degree of certainty or attitude toward the event.

There are different models of sentence aspect, but a broad division is normally made between perfective (in which the situation is viewed as completed) and imperfective (in which the situation is viewed as ongoing or incomplete).

Zeno Vendler (1921–2009) categorized situations into four types on the basis of their aspectual composition: **states**, which have duration; **activities**, which have duration and a change of state; **accomplishments**, which have duration and an inherent end point; and **achievements**, which have an inherent end point but no duration. These situation types provides a common point of reference in studies of verbal aspect.

The study of meaning above the level of the sentence or proposition is usually considered the domain of **pragmatics**, which is concerned with the encoding and interpretation of meaning in conversational interaction. Pragmatics analyzes **speech acts**—utterances made by speakers in a conversational context—to examine the linguistic strategies that speakers use to fulfill particular communicative needs (such as thanking, requesting, greeting) and to infer the speaker's beliefs about and attitudes toward what they are saying. For example, a speaker of English who wants to request something usually does not use a direct imperative ("Tell me the time!") but instead asks indirectly ("Do you have the time?"). Note that in such cases, although the indirect request is posed as a yes/no question, an answer such as "Yes" would be inappropriate. This mismatch between the linguistic structure and its conversational function is known as **conventional implicature**, as the function is implied rather than overt, but speakers and hearers share an understanding of the conventional interpretation of its meaning. Pragmatics involves uncovering the implicit meaning of utterances in context rather than the meaning of words or sentences in isolation.

2.2 WHAT IS SOCIOLINGUISTICS?

The preceding section outlined what is generally referred to as "core linguistics", which deals with the structural aspects of language: phonetics, phonology, morphology, syntax and semantics. Despite Saussure's recognition of language as a social fact, the main concern of core linguistics as developed in the 20th and 21st centuries has been to make explicit the knowledge of language that speakers carry around in their brains, autonomous from the "external" considerations of its use in social interaction.

In the 1960s, some linguists became concerned that other aspects of language were being ignored by core linguistics and that an understanding of language required studying not only the internal knowledge of language but also its usage.

In contrast, sociolinguistics seeks to understand how language is used in interaction among speakers, how aspects of language take on social functions, such as constructing and expressing elements of social identity, and how language structure is influenced by aspects of the social context.

Just as the term *linguistics* subsumes a number of different approaches to the study of language, the term *sociolinguistics* encompasses approaches that differ not only in terms of the theoretical or methodological assumptions that they make, but also in terms of what they view as the appropriate level of studying language in its social context. While the exact number of the different flavors of sociolinguistics is a matter of some dispute (and will depend on who you talk to), in this book I will distinguish between three general approaches that differ according to three dimensions:

- *Object of study*: Language structure or contexts of language use.
- *Scale of analysis*: Micro (small-scale interaction) or macro (large-scale social patterns).
- *Type of analysis*: Quantitative or qualitative.

This division should in no way be interpreted to mean that one object, scale or type of analysis is better than another, nor that there is no overlap between the different approaches. Each approach uses different tools to answer different types of question about language in its social context, and it is common for sociolinguists working in a community or on a research question to approach their research using multiple perspectives.

2.2.1 Linguistic Anthropology: The Ethnography of Speaking

Linguistic anthropology, which can be characterized as "micro" and qualitative in its approach, has its roots in anthropology, particularly in the fieldwork-based anthropology developed in North America in the 20th century. This approach was prefigured by Bronislaw Malinowski's (1884–1942) research on the Trobriand Islands (now part of Papua New Guinea) in the early 20th century, but it achieved greater use among American anthropologists and linguists who were concerned with documenting the disappearing indigenous cultures and languages of North America. Led by Franz Boas (1858–1942) and his students such as Edward Sapir (1884–1939), the goal of such research was to develop a complete description of the language (a *grammar*) as well as a comprehensive description of the culture (an *ethnography*).

During the development of sociolinguistics as a subfield of linguistics in the 1960s, the ethnography of speaking (which was more specifically linguistic than an ethnography of communication) approach was pioneered by Dell Hymes (1927–2009). According to his seminal paper (1962/1968: 102), the goal of sociolinguistic research was to develop a description of "the ethnographic patterning of the uses of speech in a community". The ethnographic nature of this research involves participant observation, in which the sociolinguist attempts to understand the structure of the language and culture from the insider's perspective (*emic*) rather than the outsider's perspective (*etic*), however "objective" the latter may be, by not only observing people's behaviour but also participating in the daily life of the community.

For Hymes, the basic unit of linguistic-ethnographic analysis was the **speech event**, a culturally significant activity in which language plays a role. Observing different occurrences of the same speech event (e.g. a wedding) allows the ethnographer to understand the important linguistic components of the event. Each speech event may be considered to belong to a type of speech event that can be distinguished (and often named) in cultural or social terms. Analyzing the speech event involves making multiple observations in its context of use. Hymes subdivided speech events into different components, such as its purpose or outcome, its setting, the participants and their respective roles, and so on. By changing its components (e.g. changing the locale of a wedding from a church to a park), participants can change the nature of the speech event. This type of **componential analysis** is common in other studies of linguistic anthropology, such as understanding the relationships encoded in kinship terms and terms of address. More generally, the ethnographic approach to the study of language in its social context can be useful for understanding general conventions or norms of interaction. Discourse analysis attempts to make explicit the conventions of conversation that participants implicitly understand.

2.2.2 Sociology of Language

Another approach to the study of language in its social context may be considered *macro*, examining large-scale societal patterns of language use, particularly their interaction with questions of multilingual societies and the social-symbolic function of language within these societies. This approach, which I will refer to as "the sociology of language", is most generally identified with the name of Joshua Fishman (1926–2015). Fishman (1968) distinguishes two different questions, which he characterizes as *descriptive* and *dynamic*:

- Descriptive: Who speaks which language (or dialect) to whom, when and to what end?
- Dynamic: What accounts for changes in the social organization of language use?

In contrast with linguistic anthropology, which examines the use of language by participating in and observing speech events, the sociology of language relies on data collected through large-scale surveys, either constructed specifically for the purposes of understanding language use or for other purposes, such as censuses distributed by government bodies.

One dimension of language use particularly relevant to the sociology of language is what people think about language, and what they think they are doing when they use language. People have very deep-seated views on languages and their speakers and how they should (and should not) be used. Clearly, these views have real-world consequences: views about language can determine whether particular languages merit being taught in the educational systems, and views about speakers of particular languages (or varieties) can determine whether you rent accommodation to those speakers or hire them to do a job. These views also affect how speakers themselves use the language, and over time these views may even have an effect on the structure of the language.

Human beings, as social creatures, have to make a number of assumptions about the world in order to function. Some of these assumptions are based on previous or current experience, but some are also filtered through **ideology**, the system of social and cultural beliefs that allow people to make sense of the world. Language ideology is the set of beliefs that people have about language and linguistic behaviour. While some beliefs may be accessible, such that people can make explicit or metalinguistic comments about it, much of language ideology is implicit. People may not be able to articulate exactly what they believe about language, but it may emerge in their discourse around other topics, in their reactions to other people or their linguistic behaviour, or they may exhibit these beliefs through their own linguistic behaviour. The average person is probably most familiar with **prescriptive** ideologies of language, which view certain forms of language and linguistic behaviour as "good", "correct" or "proper", and others as "bad", "incorrect" or "improper" (or even "sloppy" or "corrupt"). This ideology prevails in many cultures and societies and is often not only acquired as part of the child's socialization but also promoted through schools and official bodies such as language academies. The goal of prescriptive ideology is to regulate linguistic behaviour, prescribing "good" language and discouraging "bad" language. In contrast, descriptive ideology views language as a form of behaviour that is neither "good" nor "bad" in itself, but that people engage in for particular reasons. The goal of descriptivism is not to regulate linguistic behaviour, but rather to describe it and to understand the reasons that people engage in such behaviour. This is the ideology adopted in linguistics, whose goal is to understand the linguistic system in the individual speaker's head, and how that speaker uses language.

Language ideologies are reflected in the attitudes that people have toward the object of those beliefs, which can be studied in different ways. Studies of language attitudes divide them into three different components. The **cognitive** component has to do with the knowledge or beliefs that people have about language, whether or not that knowledge is directly accessible by the individual. The **conative** component concerns actions, or the reflection of language attitudes in linguistic behaviour. The **affective** component concerns the evaluation that individuals make of other people or their linguistic behaviour, as revealed through emotional reactions. Different approaches to the study of language attitudes address these different components by measuring evaluations or ratings of language (varieties) and attitudes toward speakers and through language choice and usage. Because these attitudes may not be accessible to inference or introspection, they often require methods of indirect elicitation.

Studies of language attitudes make use of different methods. Content analysis involves examining the public treatment of language in media or political discourse, though it may also take the form of ethnographic analysis (participant observation). Attitudes may be elicited directly, either through the qualitative analysis (e.g. the use of case studies or interviews) or through quantitative analysis (e.g. the use of questionnaires, using either open or closed questions). More commonly, studies of language attitudes rely on indirect measurements; rather than asking the individual directly for their views, their attitudes may be inferred from their response to particular tasks.

The most common method of indirectly measuring language attitudes is the **matched-guise test**, developed by Wallace Lambert (1922–2009) and Howard Giles in the 1960s in Montreal. The matched-guise test involves recording the same people speaking in different "guises" (languages or accents), playing these guises in random order to listeners and asking the listeners to rate each voice they hear according to different characteristics such as trustworthiness, friendliness, kindness, and so on. Because the only information available to the listeners is the language or accent of the voice, their reaction can only be based on their attitudes toward people who speak that way. An interesting result of this research is the finding that listeners often rate speakers of their own language or accent negatively on personal attributes associated with power or prestige but positively on attributes associated with personal integrity and friendliness. This result offers an explanation for why speakers of disadvantaged languages or accents experience a high degree of linguistic insecurity while still continuing to speak that way.

Another method for indirectly studying language attitudes is perceptual dialectology, first developed in Japan and the Netherlands but introduced to North American sociolinguistics by Dennis Preston and his students and associates. Perceptual dialectology differs from traditional dialectology (see below) in its concern not so much with the geographic distribution of features but with the perceptions that ordinary people have with dialectal differences and their distribution.

2.2.3 Language Variation and Change

Variation is part of language: whenever we speak, we must adhere to the rules of our language to be understood, but we also make choices about how to pronounce certain sounds and about which word or grammatical construction to use. These choices help to shape the language we use, and they also tell those who hear us something about ourselves. In some cases, they may even influence the choices that other speakers of the language make.

What do we mean by "variation"? In a trivial sense, variation obviously exists between different languages: when you learn another language, a lot of the effort involved is memorizing the different sound–meaning pairs and the (sometimes very) different rules about how words and sentences are put together. Variation also exists within the same language, although we tend not to think of it as variation, because we can usually provide explanations for apparent variation in terms of differences in meaning or in the linguistic context. In many cases it may be difficult, if not impossible, to find a change in meaning or a difference in the linguistic context that would allow us to distinguish between differences in meaning. Such situations are usually labeled as *free variation*, which implies that the choice is completely random.

In the 1960s, William Labov (1927–) began to examine these questions more systematically. His study of Martha's Vineyard (Labov 1963) examined variation in the diphthongs /ay/ and /aw/ in the English spoken on this Massachusetts island. He expanded this work in studies of the Lower East Side, New York City (Labov 1966) and African American youth in Harlem (Labov, Cohn, Robins and Lewis 1968), and his students and colleagues began to carry out similar studies in other cities, such as Panama City (Cedergren 1973), Montreal (Sankoff and Cedergren 1972), Norwich (Trudgill 1974) and Belfast (Milroy and Milroy 1978). Labov's approach was to study so-called "free" variation more systematically by examining the correlation of variant forms with elements of the linguistic and social context. Rather than assuming that every difference in linguistic form is meaningful, this approach assumes that variation is an inherent property of language, and that linguistic analysis should take variation into account rather than trying to eliminate it.

The study of sociolinguistic variation and change rests on the construct of the *variable*, which can be defined generally as "different ways of saying the same thing". Any time that a speaker has a choice between two or more linguistic forms to express (roughly) the same meaning, we have the possibility of a sociolinguistic variable. The first part of this definition involves the "different ways", the *variants*. For example, you have probably noticed that speakers of English can produce the final syllable of the word *singing* with either a velar [ɪŋ] or an alveolar [ɪn] (known colloquially as "dropping the *g*"). This variation suggests that we have a sociolinguistic variable (*-ing*) with two variants, *-ing* and *-in'*. Variables can be found in different parts of the linguistic system: phonetic or phonological, lexical, morphological and syntactic. The second part of the definition of a variable, "the same thing", requires that we determine what the variants have in common. If variants represent the speaker's choice among different linguistic forms, where is this choice possible? This question constitutes the central methodological problem of the study of socio-linguistic variation, that of defining the *variable context* (or the *envelope of variation*). This step in the analysis is important because it will determine the rest of the analysis. Defining the variable context involves figuring out which forms alternate with each other. The principle of accountability requires that we take into consideration not only the linguistic form of interest to us, but also all of the other forms with which it covaries.

Defining a variable context for grammatical variables is more controversial. For example, speakers of English sometimes refer to the future with the modal verb *will* (*It will rain tomorrow*) or with the periphrastic construction *be going to* (*It's going to rain tomorrow*), which suggests that there is a variable (FUTURE). But are these really "different ways of saying the same thing", or do they have subtle semantic differences? Rather than trying to determine whether both forms are semantically equivalent, we could instead identify a particular linguistic function (here, the future) and note all the different forms that convey that function, using the conditioning by linguistic factors to further refine the analysis.

Defining the variable context guides the extraction of occurrences (or tokens) of the variable from the data, whether the data be recorded speech, transcriptions of recordings or historical or online texts. The most common method of data collection in the study of sociolinguistic variation is the *socio-linguistic interview*, in which speakers are encouraged to talk for an hour or two on topics of interest to them, and may be asked to read passages of writing or lists of words containing the variables of interest (Labov 1984; Tagliamonte 2006b).

More important than calculating the overall rate of each variant is understanding the contribution made by elements of the linguistic and social context to the choice of variant, by comparing rates of variants across (social or linguistic) contexts. Unlike in core linguistic analysis, rather than looking for complementary distribution of variants (all vs. nothing), the goal is to identify changes in rates across different contexts (more vs. less). Because of this focus on changes in rates, the analysis of sociolinguistic variation is necessarily quantitative.

We can divide explanations into two broad types: those *external* to the linguistic system and those *internal*. Language-external explanations involve what we might call the *socio-symbolic* uses of variation; that is, the indication of membership in different social groups, such as social class, sex/gender, level of education, ethnicity and so on. Obviously, a large proportion of phonological variation conveys these functions (for example, people can tell a lot about my sex, my age and where I grew up by my pronunciation), and in fact most studies of phonological variation tend to concentrate on this type of conditioning. Variation may also be conditioned by lexical features (such as the effects of individual words or word-classes), phonetic and phonological factors (such as the preceding and following segment or the stress of the syllable), and grammatical factors (such as morphological status or structure, syntactic role, and the presence of other constituents in the sentence). These are all language-internal explanations.

The distribution of variants across factors is examined by calculating the rate of each variant within each factor and comparing frequencies across factors within the same factor group. If these frequencies are different, how do we know whether these differences are meaningful or whether they simply reflect random "noise" in the data or the effect of some other factor that has not been considered? Answering this question requires a test of *statistical significance*, which determines how likely it is that the *null hypothesis* (H_0; none of the factors tested are affecting the variable) is true. If the difference between *expected values* (what the distribution of data would look like if the null hypothesis were true) and *observed values* (the actual distribution of data) is big enough, we can conclude that the variation is meaningful. The probability that the null hypothesis is true is expressed as a value of p: the lower the p-value, the less likely it is that the observed distribution of data is due to chance. The usual cutoff point for deciding statistical significance for p is 5%. So the statement "p is less than 5%" ($p < 5\%$ or $p < .05$) means that there is a less than 5% chance that the null hypothesis is true, and we can be reasonably confident that the difference in rate between factor groups is statistically significant.

While tests of statistical significance are useful for evaluating the significance of individual factors, analyzing sociolinguistic variation normally involves multiple hypotheses about the contextual influences on the variation. Techniques of multivariate analysis assess the individual contribution of each factor to the observed variation when all of the factors are considered together. A common statistical tool is the VARBRUL family of computer programs (especially Gold-Varb [Sankoff, Tagliamonte and Smith 2012]) and, more recently, Rbrul (Johnson 2009), which use binomial logistic regression. In this procedure, variation is modeled as a choice between applying (or not applying) a variable "rule", with an estimate of the relative contribution that each factor makes to the application of the rule. Calculating the overall probability that the rule applies (the *input* or *corrected mean*) and the overall *log likelihood*, which provides a baseline value of how well the current model predicts the observed distribution of data, each factor receives an estimate of its contribution to the application value, expressed as a *factor weight* (a probability that ranges between 0 and 1 and is centered on .5, such that a value above .5 favors application and a value below .5 disfavors application) or a *logodds* (a numerical coefficient that may be positive or negative, centered on 0, with positive values favoring application and negative values disfavoring). Statistical significance is determined by a stepwise procedure, in which the factor groups are successively added and then subtracted from the model, with each model's log likelihood calculated and compared for significant changes. Thus, the program looks for the configuration of factors that provides the best fit to the observed distribution of variants. The relative strength of each factor group can be expressed in the order in which each factor group is selected as significant (i.e. the factor group that provides the biggest change in log likelihood) or by comparing the *range* of each factor group (the difference between the largest and smallest factor weight, or logodds, in each factor group). Note that logistic regression requires nominal variants. For continuous-variant measurements (such as F1 and F2 measurements for vowel variables), *linear* regression (as implemented in Rbrul) is more appropriate.

SUMMARY

This chapter has been intended to provide readers with a basic understanding of the terms and methods used in linguistics and sociolinguistics.

Linguistics is a scholarly discipline that is concerned with the study of language and that overlaps with other disciplines that study aspects of human physiology, psychology and social behavior. Phonetics, which concerns the production of speech sounds by the human vocal apparatus, can be studied from articulatory (impressionistic) or acoustic (instrumental) perspectives. Phonology concerns the way that sounds are organized within language, centered on the contrastive unit of the phoneme and its allophonic forms. Morphology studies the structures of words and the relation between sound and meaning, expressed as morphemes and their allomorphic forms. Syntax examines the structures of sentences and their constituent categories, phrases and clauses, as well as the rules that govern word order and movement of constituents within the sentence. Semantics and pragmatics study the expression and interpretation of meaning in language. Semantics can be concerned with the meaning of individual words or that of sentences or propositions, while pragmatics concerns meaning in conversational interaction.

Sociolinguistics is a branch of linguistics that concerns the study of language in its social context. I distinguished between three different approaches to sociolinguistics, depending on their focus of study and the level of analysis: linguistic anthropology (or the ethnography of speaking), the sociology of language and language variation and change. The last approach is the main focus of this book, so we defined terms such as the variable and the variable context and discussed some of the methodological issues involved in conducting quantitative analysis of linguistic behavior.

Readers who have consulted this chapter should be able to follow the discussion in the remainder of the book, especially the linguistic details of Chapters 4 to 7.

3

The Origins and Development
of Canadian English

3.0 INTRODUCTION

In order to understand where any dialect of English came from and why it has the shape that it does, it is necessary to understand what we might call its "language-external" history; that is, rather than focusing on its structural elements, we focus on the history of its speakers. Why is English spoken so widely throughout the world, and in so many different ways? In the case of Canadian English, this requires an understanding of how English spread throughout the world and the sequence of events that led to this remarkable situation.

Before beginning this discussion, I'll note that the word *dialect* is problematic from a linguistic perspective. Apart from the negative connotations of the word (e.g. it is often used disparagingly for ways of speaking that differ from the written standard or that are used by people from more peripheral regions or lower social classes), the distinction between *dialect* and *language* is not made on the basis of purely linguistic considerations (such as similarities in vocabulary, pronunciation and grammar) or mutual intelligibility (i.e. the ability of speakers of each dialect to understand each other), but primarily because of social, cultural and political attitudes. To cite two commonly used examples, the Scandinavian languages (Danish, Norwegian and Swedish) are structurally very similar and mutually intelligible, yet the dialects of Chinese (i.e. its spoken forms, such as Cantonese and Mandarin) differ structurally in a number of ways and are not mutually intelligible. For these reasons, although I will often use the word *dialect*, in keeping with the literature on the topic, I will also use the more neutral term *variety* as much as possible to refer to forms of language that differ socially or regionally.

3.1 THE ORIGIN AND SPREAD OF ENGLISH DIALECTS

English itself began as a dialect, or a group of dialects, spoken by people from what is now the Netherlands, northern Germany and Denmark. In the 5th and 6th centuries AD, these people, who spoke Germanic languages (related to such modern languages as German, Dutch and Frisian), migrated to and gradually conquered most of Britain, an island that had been ruled by the Roman Empire and was populated by speakers of Celtic languages (the ancestors of today's Welsh and Gaelic). Over the next several centuries their languages developed into a set of dialects that are now referred to as "Anglo-Saxon" or "Old English". The lack of mixing between the speakers of Old English and the Celtic speakers they pushed to the fringes of the island meant that there was little Celtic influence on the development of English at that time. The greatest influence on Old English was exerted by the Vikings, who spoke Old Norse, and who occupied a large part of Britain under the Danelaw between the 9th and 11th centuries. With the conquest by the French-speaking Normans in 1066, French became the language of the court and nobility. At this point, Old English gave way to Middle English, the language used by Geoffrey Chaucer in poems such as *The Canterbury Tales*, written toward the end of the 14th century, by which time English had been reestablished as the language of the court. Middle English developed into Modern English beginning in the mid to late 15th century. Early Modern English, the language used by William Shakespeare, was still characterized by dialectal variation, but a written standard (based mostly on the English spoken in London, the capital) and a body of literature was beginning to be developed.

What is remarkable is that between the years 1500 and 2000 a language spoken by a million or so people in a marginal European island has become perhaps the most widely spoken language in human history. How did this come about?

English first began by dominating the British Isles. The principalities that made up Wales were conquered by England in the 13th century, followed by political union in 1536. Ireland was conquered by England, first by the (French-speaking) Normans (1169) and then by the (English-speaking) Tudors (1542). England never conquered Scotland, but the two kingdoms' crowns were unified under King James (I in England but VI in Scotland) in 1603, with political union following in 1707. Like Middle and Modern English, the Scots language was a descendant of the dialects of Old English. Scots competed with Gaelic and French in Scotland, but by the end of the 14th century it had become the dominant language of that kingdom. With the political union of the British Isles under England came increasing use of English for official purposes (law and trade) and a concomitant proscription of other languages (Gaelic in Scotland, Welsh in Wales and Irish in Ireland).

English began to spread out from the British Isles over the course of the 16th and 17th centuries, as England entered into the European enterprise of colonization and conquest, competing with other European powers, first Spain and France, then the Netherlands and Portugal. Although English explorers began to discover overseas lands in the 16th century (such as Newfoundland), the first permanent English-speaking settlement outside of the British Isles was at Jamestown, Virginia, in 1607, with other settlements along the eastern seaboard of North America to follow. English colonies were also founded in the Caribbean, at St Kitts (1623) and Barbados (1625–27), followed by other islands throughout the 17th and 18th centuries. Colonies in central and South America were also established, though their control passed back and forth between England (later, Britain) and the other European powers.

While Britain established settlement colonies and plantations in North America and the Caribbean, its entry into trade in Asia (India, China and the East Indies) and Africa was characterized more by commercial and military colonies. British control of the Indian subcontinent began with trade colonies founded under the auspices of the East India Company in 1757, though India was made a colony of the British crown in 1858. Britain's entry into Asia and the Pacific led to the discovery of lands such as Australia, first settled as a penal colony in 1788, and New Zealand, settled in 1840. The need to safeguard commercial routes from Asia around Africa prompted the seizure of the Cape of Good Hope in 1806, with later conquests of indigenous and Boer (Dutch) territories, leading to the formation of the colony of South Africa. Trade colonies were also established in the Malay peninsula (Penang in 1786, Singapore in 1819 and Malacca in 1824), in Burma (1826) and on Hong Kong island (1842). In the late 19th century, Britain was also involved with other European powers in the "scramble for Africa", acquiring territories in West Africa (Nigeria, Ghana and Sierra Leone) and East Africa (Kenya, Zambia and Zimbabwe).

The American Revolution removed most of the English-speaking colonies in North America from British control, and the 19th and 20th centuries saw an increasing degree of political autonomy from Britain in the other settlement colonies (Canada, Australia and New Zealand). Most of Ireland became independent from Britain in the early 20th century, and after the Second World War other overseas British colonies began to follow suit. The former British colonies of Asia and Africa underwent a process of decolonization, but the English language continued to play a role in these new countries to different degrees, either as a (co-)official language or as a language of higher education. Although the British Empire gradually dissolved and Britain's worldwide power waned, the rise of the United States of America (another English-speaking country) as a superpower guaranteed the maintenance and worldwide spread of the English language, though increasingly through military and economic power rather than through colonialism and conquest.

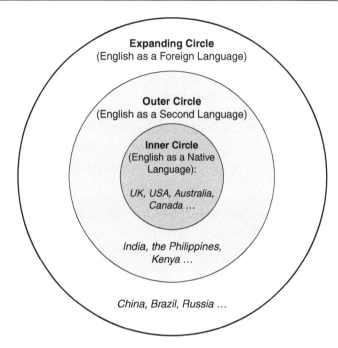

FIGURE 3.1 The circles of World English

Source: Adapted from Kachru 1992.

The idea of "World English" was proposed by the linguist Braj Kachru in the 1990s. In this model, World English can be viewed as an international set of interrelated dialects or varieties that can be characterized in three concentric circles (see Figure 3.1). In the Inner Circle, English is spoken (by most of the population) as a native language. The Inner Circle would include the former settlement colonies, now countries such as the United Kingdom, Canada, the United States, Australia, New Zealand and South Africa. In the Outer Circle, English is primarily spoken as a second language. The Outer Circle includes the former colonies of Britain and the United States, countries such as India, the Philippines, Kenya, Nigeria, and so on. Finally, in the Expanding Circle, English is spoken as a foreign language. These are countries with no English-speaking settlement or colonial history, but where English is making increasing inroads as a language of international communication and trade. The Expanding Circle includes countries such as Russia, China, Japan and Brazil.

3.2 PRINCIPLES OF NEW DIALECT FORMATION

The previous section outlined the language-external factors leading to the origins and spread of the English language around the world. In this section, we will focus on the development of the linguistic characteristics of the language as it spread. Why do the dialects of English have the form that they do? Any account of their development must take into consideration two opposing tendencies of language change, what David Crystal (2004) has called *centripetal* (or conservative) and *centrifugal* (or innovative) forces: centripetal forces act to maintain the unity of different ways of speaking as dialects of the same language, whereas centrifugal forces lead to greater differentiation of dialects.

The most common way of depicting relationships between languages (or dialects or varieties) is the *family tree*. By analogy with biology or genealogy, the family-tree model views languages as organisms that have *parents* that they descend from (although, unlike most biological organisms, they only have one parent). As illustrated in Figure 3.2, Language A gives rise to two different languages, B and C, whose similarities can be traced back to their common inheritance from the parent Language A. For example, as outlined in the previous section, the varieties of English spoken in the British Isles 500 years ago gave rise to the current varieties of English spoken in the British Isles, in the United States, in Canada, and so on. The family-tree model operates on the assumption that language spreads through a process of *transmission* (or *linguistic descent*), which William Labov (2007: 346) defines as an "unbroken sequence of native-language acquisition by children". Under this process, children acquire the forms and patterns of their parents (and other members of the community in which they are raised), faithfully replicate them and then serve as linguistic models for the next generation.

However, the family tree is not the only model of language relationships: language change can also spread by *diffusion* from one dialect to another (B → C or C → B), from the mother dialect to the daughters (A→B or A→C) or from the daughters to the mother (B→A or C→A). For example, the *r*-less pronunciation now associated with British English arose at a time after the North American colonies were founded, but began diffusing to the eastern ports of Boston, New York and Charleston. The process of diffusion obviously requires contact between communities (or between speakers from different communities), which normally involves contact between adults rather than transmission from adult to child. As William Labov (2007) points out, the difference in the agents of transmission and diffusion may result in different degrees of replication of features and patterns, depending on the intensity and

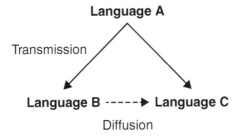

FIGURE 3.2 Illustration of the family-tree and wave models of language similarities

duration of contact between languages: more faithful replication with transmission, less faithful replication with diffusion. The degree of transmission
and diffusion may also be affected by isolation whether physical, geographic,
linguistic or social.

Some similarities in related languages cannot be accounted for by either
transmission or diffusion. As Edward Sapir (1921: 172) noted, there is a tendency for languages that trace their source to a common parent but have not
been in contact with each other to develop in similar ways. For example, both
Canadian English and Australian English feature the flapping of /t/ between
vowels, despite not having developed in contact with each other. This process
of *drift* (independent but parallel innovation) is difficult to account for via
the model shown in Figure 3.2, and may require us to appeal to universals of
language change or to tendencies inherent in the parent language.

Centrifugal forces of language change account for differences among varieties of the same language, which over time may become so great that these
varieties can come to be viewed as different languages. For example, the languages of Europe that are now classed as Romance languages (French, Italian,
Spanish, Portuguese, Romanian and so on) were originally regional varieties
of Latin spoken in different parts of the Roman Empire that diverged over
time. Centrifugal forces help to explain some of the differences between the
circles of World English proposed by Kachru (Figure 3.2). A number of theories have been developed to account for differences in the development of new
dialects (some specifically within the context of English; e.g. Mufwene 2001, 2008;
Schneider 2007; Trudgill 2004), but they converge on a number of points.

Most new dialects arise in conditions of colonization, in which a population of speakers of a language moves into a new region. A first consideration in
new-dialect formation is the initial conditions of the settlement: whether the
settlers were the first arrivals in the region, where they came from and what
dialects they already spoke. New arrivals to a region where there is already a
population that speaks the same language are more likely to assimilate to local
ways of speaking than to develop a new dialect. In a situation that Peter Trudgill
(2004) refers to as a *tabula rasa* ("clean slate"), new arrivals to a region where
there is no other substantial preexisting population that speaks the same language may set the linguistic patterns for future arrivals, under what Salikoko
Mufwene (2001) calls the "founder principle" (or the "founder effect"). However, the strength of the founder effect depends on a number of other considerations, having to do with sheer numbers of speakers (demographics) and with
social conditions, such as the degree of inequality and segregation between the
settlers and other populations. If subsequent arrivals increase the population
only gradually, the founder effect is likely to hold, because of the above-noted
tendency for new arrivals to assimilate to local ways of speaking; in contrast,
large-scale immigration by speakers of other dialects may minimize or over-
turn the founder effect. Another consideration is the *type* of colony (Mufwene

2001). *Fort* or *trade colonies*, such as those founded in Asia and Africa, were established for specific, limited purposes (usually, defense, conquest or trade) and were characterized by limited input of European populations and a restriction of communication with other populations to specific functions. The *plantation colonies* established in the Caribbean and the Pacific between the 17th and 19th centuries for large-scale farming of specific crops, such as sugar and cotton, involved a small and limited number of European managers or settlers and importation of much larger populations of slaves or indentured laborers. In these colonies, there was a large demographic imbalance among speakers of different languages, a high degree of social inequality and segregation and varying levels of communication between the different populations. The *settlement colonies* founded in North America, Australia, New Zealand and (parts of) South Africa involved large-scale immigration and permanent settlement from the British Isles. Settlement colonies were characterized by a higher degree of native-speaker transmission across generations, while colonies with a higher proportion of non-native speaker immigrants and more limited communication would have entailed processes of second-language acquisition and language shift by the immigrant groups, with more radical linguistic restructuring, leading to the simplification and overgeneralization of linguistic rules.

Even in colonial situations where native-speaker transmission was maintained, the resulting dialect would have been influenced by the mix of dialect features that the settlers brought with them to the new community, what Salikoko Mufwene (2001) has referred to as the "feature pool". As in population genetics, the new dialect would result from a combination of the initial feature pool and the (social and linguistic) conditions that favoured the selection of particular features. If the settlers were relatively homogeneous in terms of the dialect area from which they originated (*monogenesis*), the new dialect would likely resemble the old one. However, if the settlers' origins were dialectally heterogeneous, the initial feature pool would be characterized by a high degree of interdialectal variation. The emergence of the new dialect would then involve stabilization of this variation in different ways.

The most likely outcome of interdialectal variation is some degree of *dialect leveling* (or *koinéization*, from the Greek word *koiné*, meaning "common"), in which certain dialect features survive and others disappear, though the exact linguistic outcome of dialect leveling depends on social and linguistic conditions. Demographics is one consideration: linguistic features or patterns that are associated with a dialect that is spoken by a majority of the settlers has a greater chance of survival than those that are spoken by a minority. Another consideration is how *marked* a linguistic feature is: for example, certain sounds are more unusual in English dialects (such as the velar fricative [x] or front rounded vowels, both of which are found in some dialects of Scottish English) and certain past-tense forms are more irregular (such as *et* for *ate* or *riz* for *rose*). Features that are linguistically marked tend to be lost, even if they occur in the speech of a large number of settlers. Another possible resolution of dialectal variation is the *reallocation* of dialect features (Trudgill 2004), either as social or stylistic variants (*functional* or *social* reallocation) or as variants that differ in their linguistic conditioning (*structural* or *linguistic* reallocation). For example, Peter Trudgill (2006) suggests that the phonological context of Canadian Raising (before voiceless consonants; see Chapter 5, p. 82) arose as a structural reallocation of variants introduced by Scottish settlers. Finally, Roger Lass (1990) has noted a curious effect in the development of new dialects of English that he calls "swamping", which is the tendency for southeastern (i.e. London) features to be favoured in new-dialect formation, regardless of the degree of demographic input from the southeast. Swamping may be related to the importance of linguistic ideology in maintaining or developing norms of language use, either informally (through language attitudes) or formally (through institutional and educational means). The stabilization of dialects (or "focusing", to use Le Page and Tabouret-Keller's [1985] term) in most colonies began as *exonormative* (Schneider 2007); that is, they looked to Britain for linguistic norms. As the colonies developed political and cultural autonomy from Britain, the development of local norms led to *endonormative* stabilization.

Different models of new-dialect formation all agree on three main generalizations. First, no two colonies have exactly the same history: each colony was subject to different social, historical and demographic factors, and they would have passed through different stages of new-dialect formation at different rates. Second, the social and linguistic factors discussed above are *probabilistic*: linguistic outcomes cannot be predicted beforehand but may only be understood in retrospect. Finally, language-external considerations are paramount in accounting for the shape of a new dialect: even given the same mix of demographic and linguistic features, no two dialects will be linguistically identical.

3.3 THE HISTORY OF CANADIAN ENGLISH

Having provided a general history of the origins of English and its spread around the world, and having outlined the important considerations involved in accounting for the emergence of new dialects, in this section I present a chronological account of the important historical events that were relevant to the formation of English in Canada.

3.3.1 Prerevolutionary Canada

The first human presence in what is now Canada consisted of people who migrated from Asia across the Bering land bridge between Siberia and Alaska between 7,000 and 12,000 years ago. These travelers spoke languages that, as they traveled further south, divided even further into groups or families of languages that were spread throughout North and South America. At the time of European arrival in the 16th and 17th centuries, it is estimated that up to 300 languages were spoken by about 350,000 people in the territory now contained by Canada. Most of the original population was killed off by infectious diseases and the genocidal policies of many of the settlers. Nowadays, fewer than 100 of these aboriginal (or "First Nations") languages are spoken in Canada, with small numbers of speakers, most of whom have shifted to one of the official languages, English or French.

Europeans paid sporadic or seasonal visits to the island that is now known as Newfoundland, but the first substantial European presence in mainland Canada dates to the two French colonies founded by Samuel de Champlain in the early 17th century: Acadia (Acadie), founded in 1604 (in present-day Nova Scotia, New Brunswick and Prince Edward Island [originally called Île St Jean]), and Nouvelle France ("New France", nowadays Québec), which was established in 1609 along the St Lawrence River. Although there are many French-speaking communities elsewhere in Canada, the bulk of Canada's French-speaking population still resides in these two areas.

The English presence in Canada can be traced to two original sources: the island of Newfoundland, which lies at the extreme eastern edge of northern North America, and the 13 colonies established north to south along the eastern seaboard of middle North America.

Newfoundland had been visited by Scandinavians for centuries before it was (re)discovered in 1497 by the Venetian navigator John Cabot (Zuan Chabotto) under the sponsorship of England's King Henry VII. It served as a seasonal fishery for the French, Basques, Portuguese and Spanish but was claimed for the English Crown in 1583. Permanent settlements began to be established in the 17th century, with immigration almost exclusively from southwestern England (Dorset, Devon and Cornwall) and southeastern Ireland (Waterford, Wexford, Kilkenny, Tipperary and Cork). By 1750 the permanent population was no more than about 5,000 (Clarke 2010b), though it increased to about 100,000 by 1850, with immigration continuing to come from the same sources. Due to the homogeneity of its settler input and its geographical and political isolation (until relatively recently), the linguistic characteristics of Newfoundland are quite different from those of the rest of English-speaking North America.

The 13 English-speaking colonies in mid-Atlantic North America were established gradually throughout the 17th and 18th centuries: Virginia in 1607 (although it had been unsuccessfully settled in the 16th century), Massachusetts in 1628, Maryland in 1632, Rhode Island in 1636 (originally settled as Providence), Connecticut in 1636, North and South Carolina in 1663 (originally as one colony, then divided in two in 1691), New York and New Jersey in 1664 (both originally part of the New Netherlands colony settled by the Dutch in the early 1600s), Delaware in 1664, Pennsylvania in 1681, New Hampshire in 1691 and Georgia in 1732. By the mid-1700s, the population of these colonies (excluding slaves) stood at about 1.5 million. For the most part, the colonists were English-speaking emigrants from various parts of the British Isles, although some of the colonies had already been settled by speakers of Dutch and Swedish. As shown in Figure 3.3, these English-speaking colonies were on the edge of a continent still populated predominantly by aboriginal societies, but held by France and Spain.

The course of the 18th century saw a series of European wars between Britain and France also played out in North America between the neighbouring

FIGURE 3.3 North America ca. 1750 (superimposed on current state and provincial borders)

Source: Adapted from http://commons.wikimedia.org/wiki/File:Nouvelle-France_map-en.svg.

British and French colonies (each of which was allied with different aboriginal nations). Over the course of 50 years, Britain gradually gained control over more and more North American territory.

During the War of the Spanish Succession (1701–14), French Acadia was conquered by Britain, which was allowed to keep it under the terms of the Treaty of Utrecht (1713) (though without Île Royale, later Cape Breton Island). To counter the French fortress at Louisbourg (in Île Royale), the British established the port city of Halifax in 1749, bringing in 3,000 English-speaking settlers (mainly from Britain, New England and Newfoundland) and establishing the new province of Nova Scotia. A few years later, the English-speaking settlers were followed by over 2,000 Protestant German-speaking settlers from parts of what are now Germany and Switzerland (Wynne 1987a). Although the British at first tolerated the existence of French-speaking Acadians in the province, their refusal to sign oaths of loyalty to the British Crown in the ongoing battles with France, coupled with the interest of New Englanders in obtaining Acadian land, led to the forced deportation of many Acadians to the southern British colonies and to Louisiana between 1755 and 1758. Following this deportation, their land was settled by about 8,000 "Yankee planters" from New England. By 1776, there were about 70,000 people in Nova Scotia, a third of them concentrated in Halifax, though most of the population spoke an aboriginal language (Mi'kmaq or Maliseet) or French (Wynne 1987b).

The British conquest of the eastern half of North America was complete at the end of the Seven Years' War (1755–63, also known as the French and Indian War), during which the French fortresses at Louisbourg (1758), Québec (1759) and Montréal (1760) were captured. These gains were consolidated under the terms of the Treaty of Paris (1763), in which Britain gained all the territories of French North America (except for the islands of St Pierre and Miquelon, off the southeast of Newfoundland, which are still part of France to this day)—a vast swath of land that stretched from Acadia in the northeast, through the St Lawrence River and the Great Lakes, and south through the land east of the Mississippi to the Gulf of Mexico (see Figure 3.4). Although the American colonists to the south had assumed that their new fellow-subjects of the British Crown would be assimilated into their largely Protestant and English-speaking society, the British Parliament's passage of the Quebec Act (1774) guaranteed the Quebec colonists their right to remain French-speaking and Catholic and to retain their legal system. Despite a slight influx of English speakers from the American colonies into this territory over the next 13 years, the vast majority of its 70,000 inhabitants remained French speaking.

Thus, by 1776 there were no more than 25,000 speakers of English in all of what is now Canada, with only a few hundred in the new province of Quebec (present-day Ontario and Quebec) (Orkin 1970; Wynne 1987a, 1987b).

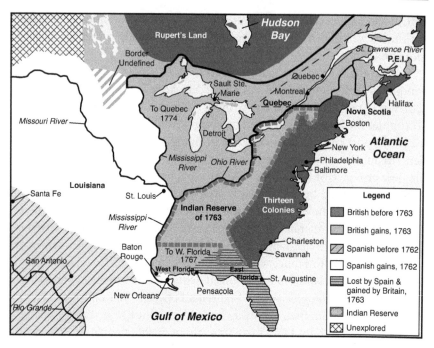

FIGURE 3.4 North America after the Treaty of Paris (1763)

Source: Adapted from http://commons.wikimedia.org/wiki/File:NorthAmerica1762-83.png.

3.3.2 The American Revolution and the Arrival of the Loyalists

In the 1760s and 1770s, disputes between the American colonists and the British government over taxation and restrictions on the expansion of the colonies into the newly acquired territories to the north and west (as well as the Quebec Act) escalated into armed rebellion. The Declaration of Independence from Britain (1776) by the Continental Congress began a seven-year war to decide the fate of the colonies. As it became clear that the rebellion was becoming a successful war of independence, many of those American colonists who did not wish to sever political ties with the mother country, who became known as "United Empire Loyalists" (or simply, "Loyalists"), were debarred from power and came under increasing attack from American Patriots. While some Loyalists were able to travel overland to Quebec via the frontiers at the Niagara and St Lawrence rivers (see Figure 3.5A), many gathered in New York City, one of the last holdouts of the British troops.

Before surrendering New York to General George Washington, the commander of the British forces, Sir Guy Carleton, negotiated the safe passage of Loyalists out of the city by sea. Many Loyalists made their way to Britain or ended up in more far-flung locales (such as the Bahamas, Jamaica and

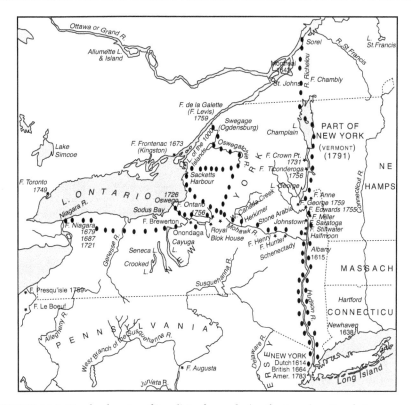

FIGURE 3.5A Overland routes of Loyalist refugees during the American Revolution

Source: Mika and Mika 1976: 122.

even India), but the main destination was the British North American provinces that had not participated in the American Revolution: Nova Scotia and Quebec.

In October and November of 1783, some 30,000 Loyalists set sail from New York City to Halifax (Jasanoff 2011; Taylor 2007). Among them were about 3,000 "Black Loyalists", most of them former slaves from Virginia and South Carolina who had heeded the proclamation by the British governor of Virginia, Lord Dunmore, that any African American slaves who helped the British resist the rebellion would be granted their freedom at the end of the war (Walker 1993).

The arrival of so many English-speaking refugees in Nova Scotia created administrative problems that were resolved by partitioning the province between the peninsula, where about 19,000 Loyalists settled, and a new province on the mainland called New Brunswick, where some 15,000 Loyalists

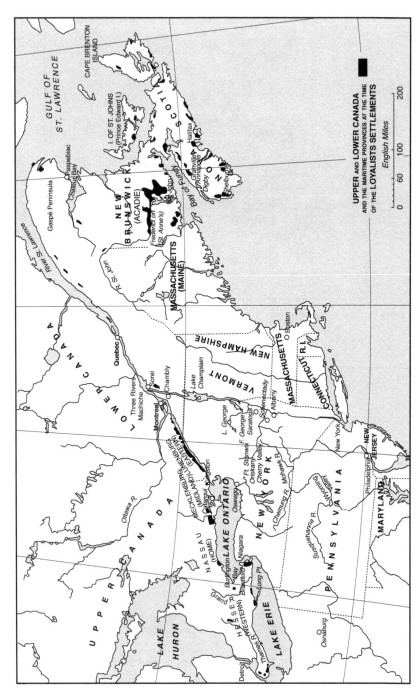

FIGURE 3.5B United Empire Loyalist settlements in British North America

Source: Mika and Mika 1976: 135.

settled (Jasanoff 2011). While most of the Loyalist settlers in peninsular Nova Scotia tended to come from Massachusetts, the origins of those who settled in New Brunswick were more mixed: some came from New England, but the majority were from the mid-Atlantic colonies (New York, New Jersey and Pennsylvania) (Wynne 1987b). A small number (500) settled in the Island of St John (renamed Prince Edward Island in 1794). The Black Loyalists experienced a certain amount of hostility from the other settlers and were settled in separate communities. By 1792, half of them volunteered to be resettled in the African colony of Freetown, Sierra Leone (Walker 1993). Thus, in 1800, the four Maritime provinces (Nova Scotia, New Brunswick, Cape Breton Island and Prince Edward Island) contained about 80,000 people, half of them English speakers, most of them hailing from New England and the mid-Atlantic colonies.

As mentioned earlier, the province of Quebec was already an overland destination for Loyalist refugees during the Revolutionary War. Between 1779 and 1784, some 6,000 Loyalists arrived, most of whom settled in the upper St Lawrence River area, establishing the town of Kingston (at the head of Lake Ontario), and around the Bay of Quinte, although there was also a settlement in the Niagara region (Jasanoff 2011). By 1785 there were about 7,000 Loyalists in the western part of the province, about half of them consisting of discharged British and German soldiers and their families or dependents, with the rest consisting of refugees who had migrated overland or who had originally sailed from New York and entered Quebec through the Maritime provinces (Knowles 1997). By 1791 the growing English-speaking population in the west (about 14,000) led the British to partition Quebec along the Ottawa River, with the eastern part becoming the (predominantly French-speaking) province of Lower Canada and the western part becoming the (predominantly English-speaking) province of Upper Canada (see Figure 3.5B).

The governor of the new province of Upper Canada was John Graves Simcoe, a British officer who had fought in the Revolutionary War, and who saw his task in the province as building an alternative Loyalist British North American society that would show the rebellious colonists to the south the errors of their ways (Craig 1963). Simcoe located the provincial capital at (Fort) York (later renamed Toronto) and concentrated on developing and settling the land in the western part of Upper Canada, where the Loyalists had not settled in any great numbers. His goal was to lure some of the American settlers who were migrating northwest from the mid-Atlantic states (New Jersey, New York and Pennsylvania) to Upper Canada.

Although the American settlers who arrived after 1791 are usually referred to as the "late Loyalists", this name is a little misleading, because their political allegiance and their motives for settling in Canada differed from those of the United Empire Loyalists. Rather than being motivated by political loyalty to the British Crown, they were enticed by Simcoe's offers of cheap land and rates of taxation that were lower than those in the newly founded United States (ironically, taxation had been one of the grievances of the American revolutionaries). Over the next 20 years, the arrival of these late Loyalists increased the population of Upper Canada from 14,000 to 70,000. They settled the north shore of Lake Ontario and the country north of York, and founded communities along the Grand and Thames rivers (Taylor 2007).

By 1812, the population of Upper Canada was estimated to be between 75,000 (Craig 1963; Dollinger 2008 says 83,000) and 100,000 (Craig 1963; Knowles 1997; Landon 1967). There were speakers of languages other than English: German was spoken along the upper St Lawrence, as well as Low German, spoken by Mennonites from New Jersey and Pennsylvania in Markham, Niagara and along the Grand River; speakers of Gaelic could be found in northeastern Upper Canada, and there were French-speaking communities along the Detroit and Ottawa rivers. However, the overwhelming majority of the population was English-speaking, consisting of the late Loyalists, followed by the United Empire Loyalists and British/Irish immigrants, with smaller numbers of Quakers from Pennsylvania and Black Loyalists.

3.3.3 The War of 1812 and Its Aftermath

In 1812, the United States, under President James Madison, declared war on Britain, citing a number of grievances having to do with restrictions on trade and sovereignty. Among the American war goals was the annexation of Canada, a task that a previous president, Thomas Jefferson, had declared to be a "matter of mere marching". Although there were some American victories in the war (such as the burning of York, for which the British retaliated by burning the new American capital of Washington), the three-year war was unsuccessful in its goal of seizing Canada. The main outcome of the war was a consolidation of American sovereignty, but it also had the unintended side effect of instilling a sense of national identity among Canadians (and perhaps the beginning of a strain of anti-Americanism that persists among Canadians to the present). Throughout the War of 1812, Britain had also been engaged in another war, fought in Europe against the French dictator Napoleon Bonaparte. When both wars ended in 1815, Britain could once again turn its attention to its North American colonies.

Although the citizens of Upper Canada had acquitted themselves well in the War of 1812, the British government worried about the extent to which the province had been settled by Americans who were not necessarily ideologically or politically sound when it came to allegiance to the British Empire. There was a concern that a continued and increasing Americanization of the population could lead to another war, or even to a second American revolution. After 1815, further immigration from the United States was discouraged.

To increase the English-speaking population of British North America, the government instead encouraged immigration from the British Isles through offers of cheap land and, in some cases, free passage across the Atlantic. Although initially unsuccessful, rising unemployment and a series of famines in Britain and Ireland in the 1840s stimulated large-scale emigration. Between 1815 and 1867, it is estimated that over a million people migrated from the British Isles to British North America (Cowan 1961, 1968; Taylor 2007). The bulk of these immigrants came not from London or the south of England, but rather from the more peripheral regions of the British Isles: northern England, Scotland and Ireland. While it is difficult to get an exact idea of the composition of settlers (the first census of British North America did not occur until 1851), one indication is given by the origins of immigrants arriving at Quebec, the main port of entry to Lower and Upper Canada. As Figure 3.6 shows, between 1829 and the 1850s immigration to Canada was dominated by arrivals from Ireland. However, this figure does not show the division of arrivals by religion: before 1845, most of the Irish immigrants were Protestant (coming from the northern counties of Ireland), and it was only after the first of the potato famines in the 1840s that the Catholic Irish immigrated in any large numbers (Brunger 1990: 254). Throughout the first half of the 19th century, the English were the second-largest immigrant group, but the numbers for "English" in Figure 3.6 include emigrants from Wales, and, as noted earlier, the majority of the English immigrants came from the north of England. Scottish immigrants constituted the third-largest group in this period, although lower-class labourers, farmers and shepherds from Scotland had already begun arriving in Canada in the 1820s, settling the Rideau River valley, the town of Perth and Lanark County.

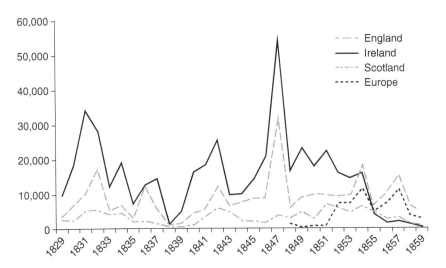

FIGURE 3.6 Arrivals at the Port of Quebec, 1829–59

Source: Based on Cowan 1961: 289, Table II.

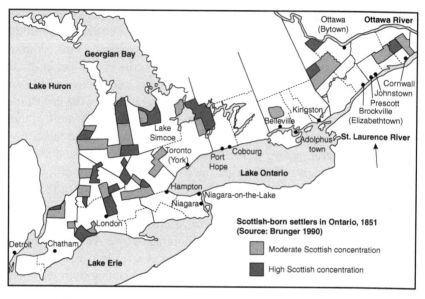

FIGURE 3.7 Scottish settlements in Upper Canada by 1851

Source: Brunger 1990: 252.

These new arrivals did not immediately integrate with the existing population of Upper Canada. In contrast with the United Empire Loyalists and the late Loyalists, who had tended to settle in already-established counties and in towns such as Kingston, York (later, Toronto) and London, the new British and Irish immigrants who arrived between 1815 and 1867 moved into previously unsettled areas of Upper Canada, although they did not settle together (Brunger 1990: 257). Most of the Scottish immigrants to Upper Canada founded communities in the unsettled southwestern area between Lakes Ontario, Erie and Huron, giving recognizably Scottish names to towns such as Fergus, Elora and Kincardine (see Figure 3.7) (Brunger 1990: 251). The Protestant Irish (who were twice as numerous as the Catholics) settled the area northwest of Toronto, founding towns such as Orangeville (Brunger 1990: 254), while the Catholic Irish tended to settle in the nonagricultural eastern areas, working in wage-labour industries such as lumber, rather than farming (Brunger 1990: 257).

Immigration in the 19th century came primarily from the British Isles, but after 1846 immigration to British North America was opened up to "Germans" (these German-speaking settlers came not only from what is now Germany but also from Austria and Hungary) and to immigrants from other areas of Europe (as can be seen in Figure 3.8), albeit in much smaller numbers. In the 1850s, the German-speaking nations of Europe lost 200,000 emigrants due to economic and agricultural problems similar to those experienced in Ireland and Britain during the same period. By 1862, over 40,000 German speakers

FIGURE 3.8 Origins of foreign-born residents of Canada, 1851–91

Source: Census of Canada. Figures before 1867 refer to Upper and Lower Canada only.

had arrived in British North America, along with almost 15,000 Scandinavians (Cowan 1961). Apart from the previously mentioned Black Loyalists who had settled in Nova Scotia, approximately 60,000 African Americans fleeing slavery through the Underground Railroad arrived in southwestern Ontario between 1820 and 1860 and settled in southwestern towns such as Windsor and Chatham, although some continued to Toronto (Bordewich 2005; Winks 1997).

Thus, the English spoken in 19th-century Canada can be seen to coexist with a smaller number of speakers of other languages (apart from the remaining aboriginal languages, there were speakers of French, German, Gaelic and Scandinavian languages).

3.3.4 Confederation and Westward Expansion

By the middle of the 19th century, the growing population of Canada showed signs of a desire for greater autonomy and participatory democracy. Rebellions took place in 1837 in both Upper and Lower Canada attempting to wrest political control of the provinces away from their oligarchical elites. Both rebellions were quickly put down, but they did lead to a widening of participation in government. Following the rebellions, Lord Durham was sent to British North America to assess whether any changes should be made to the way the provinces were governed. His *Report of the Affairs of British North America* (1838) made a number of recommendations, among them reuniting Upper and Lower Canada into a single province. In 1864, a conference debating a union of the Maritime provinces (Nova Scotia, New Brunswick and Prince Edward Island), held in Charlottetown, Prince Edward Island, was joined by delegates from Canada, and resulted in another conference in

Quebec City later that year that included Newfoundland in the discussions. In 1867 these conferences led to the British Parliament's passage of the British North America Act, which united the provinces of Canada West and East (now renamed as Ontario and Quebec, respectively), Nova Scotia and New Brunswick into the Dominion of Canada (Prince Edward Island did not join Confederation until 1873). Sir John A. MacDonald, one of the Canadian delegates to the Charlottetown and Quebec conferences, became the first prime minister. The territories of northwestern British North America (Rupert's Land and the Northwest Territories), owned by the Hudson's Bay Company since 1670, were bought by British Crown and passed on to the new government of Canada in 1869–70, which created the provinces of Manitoba (1870, though with much smaller boundaries than it has today) and British Columbia (1871). Although the Canadian government encouraged settlement in this new territory by offering free land to any man over the age of 21 who would cultivate and live on it for at least three years, this policy was not successful until the end of the 19th century, when an improvement in the economies of North America and Europe increased the demand for Canadian agricultural products such as wheat. The prime minister at that time, Sir Wilfrid Laurier, made settling the west a top priority, not only promoting immigration to Canada abroad in the British Isles and Europe, but also lifting restrictions on immigration from the United States. While arrivals from Germany and Scandinavia generally declined in this period, immigration from the British Isles increased. This period also saw the beginning of immigration from southern Europe (Italy and Greece) and eastern Europe (primarily from the Ukraine and, to a lesser extent, Russia, as well as from German-speaking parts of eastern Europe) (Kelley and Trebilcock 1998). The second-largest group of immigrants came from the United States, though many of these "American" immigrants were themselves recent arrivals from central and northern Europe. The settlement of the western provinces and territories was facilitated by the transcontinental Canadian Pacific Railway (CPR), which had been built between 1881 and 1885 in fulfillment of a promise to British Columbia when it joined Confederation. The increasing western population led to the creation of two new provinces in 1905, Saskatchewan and Alberta. Immigration to Canada only began to decline during the First World War, which obviously impeded international migration.

During this time, Newfoundland had also been gaining political autonomy from Britain. In 1832 it formed a colonial assembly and became a self-governing colony in 1854. Although it was granted the status of a Dominion in 1907, bankruptcy led to a return to colonial status until Newfoundland joined the Canadian Confederation in 1949. The large-scale immigration which characterized Canada in the late 19th and early 20th centuries largely bypassed Newfoundland.

3.3.5 Canada in the 20th Century—and Beyond

Until the First World War, Canada had remained an essentially "British" colony, with the bulk of its English-speaking population tracing its origins to the British Isles, either directly or indirectly through the United States. Over the course of the 20th century, as Canada gradually gained political autonomy from the United Kingdom, the demographic nature of the Canadian population began to change.

In the late 19th century, admitting immigrants from other European backgrounds was necessary to help ensure Canadian sovereignty by settling the lands it held, as well as filling a growing labour shortage. However, given public concerns that too much non-British immigration would dilute the white Anglo-Saxon nature of the Dominion, the Canadian government passed a number of restrictive immigration laws that persisted well into the 20th century. These laws were primarily aimed at restricting or barring immigration from visibly different racial groups. Although, as mentioned earlier, a number of African Americans had settled in British North America, either as Loyalist refugees or through the Underground Railroad, further black immigration was not encouraged (emancipation of slaves in the United States in 1865 and southern poverty during the Reconstruction era also deterred further African American immigration). During the construction of the CPR, the need for cheap labour led to railroad companies recruiting Chinese "guest workers", first from California (where many Chinese men had arrived during the gold rush of the 1850s) and later directly from Guangdong and Taiwan. However, these men were discouraged from bringing their families to Canada to settle permanently, and after the completion of the CPR in 1885 the Canadian government imposed a "head tax" of $50 (increased to $100 in 1900 and then to $500 in 1903) on each Chinese immigrant to Canada as a means of minimizing Asian immigration (Li 1998). In 1923, immigration from China was banned outright by the Chinese Immigration (or Exclusion) Act, a law that was not repealed until 1947.

Canada's political autonomy increased after the First World War. The British Parliament's passage of the Statute of Westminster (1931) granted formal equality to the other Parliaments of all self-governing Dominions within the British Empire. Although the British monarch was retained as the head of state (locally represented by a governor-general), the Canadian Parliament could pass its own laws without approval from Great Britain. The Canadian Citizenship Act was passed in 1946 and went into effect in 1947. In 1965, the Canadian government replaced its British-themed Red Ensign flag with the current Maple Leaf flag.

During the 1960s, Canada also began officially to recognize its *de facto* bilingual and increasingly multicultural nature. The Royal Commission on

Bilingualism and Biculturalism (1963–67) convened by Prime Minister Lester Pearson recommended a policy of "bilingualism within a multicultural framework". Under this policy, English and French would be recognized as official languages of the federal government. Although other languages would not be recognized as official, multiculturalism would encourage people to retain the cultural practices that they brought with them from elsewhere. This policy was enacted in the Official Languages Act (1969), and, with the repatriation of the Canadian Constitution (1982), the language laws were further enshrined in the Charter of Rights and Freedoms.

From a demographic perspective, the most significant change in Canadian government policy is undoubtedly the new Immigration Act of 1962, which removed all barriers of race, religion and country of origin from immigration. Canadian immigration was later refined into a system in which potential immigrants are awarded points for knowledge of either official language, needed skills, age and financial assets.

These changes to the act resulted in visible (and audible) changes in the ethnic, cultural and linguistic composition of the Canadian population. Figure 3.9 shows the relative proportions of origins for immigrants to Canada from 1900 to 1980. At the beginning of the 20th century, the bulk of immigration was still British, with sizeable proportions from the United States and Europe. However, a finer breakdown of the relative proportion of European immigration

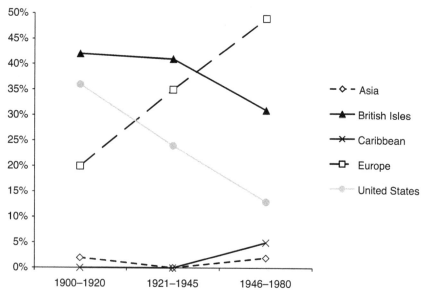

FIGURE 3.9 Relative proportions of origins of immigrants to Canada, 1900–80

Source: Adapted from McDougall 1961.

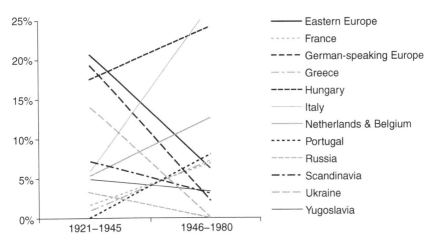

FIGURE 3.10 Relative proportions of European immigrants to Canada, 1921–80.

Source: McDougall 1961.

from 1921 to 1980, shown in Figure 3.10, reveals a marked shift in the composition of this category: declining proportions of immigrants from Scandinavia, Ukraine and Russia (groups who helped to settle the western provinces at the turn of the 20th century) and increasing proportions of immigrants from German-speaking Europe ([West] Germany, Austria and Switzerland), France and the Low Countries (the Netherlands and Belgium). However, the sharpest gains are in the relative proportions of immigrants from what is sometimes referred to as "southern Europe": Italy (primarily from Sicily and Calabria), Portugal (primarily from the Azores Islands) and Greece. In contrast with the groups who had settled the west at the turn of the century, these groups tended to settle in the larger cities, especially Montreal and Toronto.

After the 1980s, the picture of immigration to Canada begins to change even more radically. As Figure 3.11 shows, the relative proportion of immigration from the British Isles, the United States and Europe declines sharply, and we begin to see rising immigration from new areas, such as the Caribbean, the Middle East and Latin and South America. However, the steepest rise is among the category marked "Asia". If we examine the breakdown of this category more closely, as in Figure 3.12, we see that some of the groups that predominated prior to 1991 have either remained constant (the Philippines) or have declined (Hong Kong, Vietnam), while others have not only continued but have come to occupy a greater proportion of immigration from Asia (mainland China and India). Thus, within the last 30 years, the face of immigration to Canada has shifted from Europe to Asia, and in particular to two large source countries in Asia: China and India. Moreover, as was the case with the later European immigration from southern Europe after the Second World War, these newer Asian immigrants have tended to settle in the larger cities.

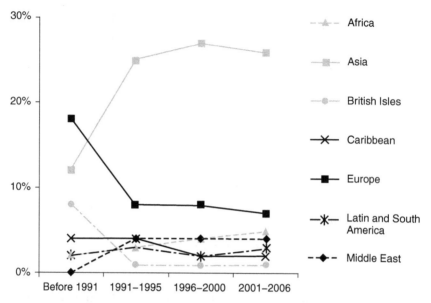

FIGURE 3.11 Relative proportion of origins of foreign-born Canadians, 1991–2006

Source: Canada Census, available at http://www.statcan.gc.ca/.

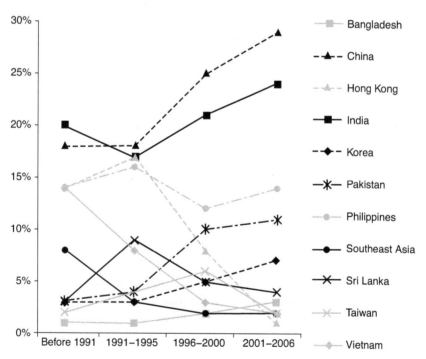

FIGURE 3.12 Relative proportions of origins of Asian-born Canadians, 1991–2006

Source: Canada Census, available at http://www.statcan.gc.ca/.

3.4 CANADIAN ENGLISH AS A NEW DIALECT

Now that we have reviewed the important historical, social and demographic events in the history of English-speaking Canada, we are in a position to examine the development of Canadian English in light of different theories of new-dialect formation. In examining this development, it is important to distinguish between the histories of the different geographical regions that served as the origins of the different English-speaking populations in Canada.

Newfoundland stands as a special case in the history of Canadian English, from both a historical and a geographic perspective. Having been settled almost exclusively from two regions of the British Isles (southwestern England and southeastern Ireland), and because settlers from these regions tended to settle together in different parts of the island, the establishment of Newfoundland English can be seen as a case of monogenesis par excellence. Current Newfoundland English shows few signs of the dialect mixture exhibited in other areas of North America (see Chapters 4–6). In addition, because of its geographical isolation and its independent political status, the large-scale immigration that characterized other parts of Canada has largely bypassed this province. Only since joining Confederation in 1949 has Newfoundland shown any signs in its English of accommodating to the national standard (Chambers 1991).

Across all regions of what is now Canada, the initial settlement of English speakers conforms with the requirements of a *tabula rasa* situation. At the time of the European arrival, there were indigenous populations who spoke aboriginal languages (Beothuk in Newfoundland, Mi'kmaq and Maliseet in Nova Scotia, various Algonquian and Iroquoian languages in Canada), but these populations were rapidly and severely reduced by diseases, warfare (with each other and with the European powers and colonists) and genocide, and thus contributed very little to the later development of English in Canada, beyond place names and a number of culturally specific words. Similarly, although there were substantial populations of French speakers in Nova Scotia and Quebec when Britain took possession of these colonies, the deportation of French speakers from Acadia and the maintenance of separate legal and linguistic rights for the French population of Quebec meant that their contribution to later development of Canadian English was also minimal, and largely restricted to the lexicon.

The establishment of the English-speaking American colonies along the eastern seaboard in the 17th and 18th centuries would already have featured contact between speakers of dialects from different parts of the British Isles, resulting in dialect leveling and the emergence of new, American dialects of English. Because of the different mixes of the input populations in each colony, there would already have been differences in the dialect spoken in each colony, which persist as regional differences to this day: the New England states, the mid-Atlantic states (New York, Pennsylvania) and the southern states.

As we have seen, parts of Nova Scotia had been settled before the American Revolution by "Yankees" from New England, who doubtless brought New England ways of speaking with them. Although there was an influx of Loyalists from both New England and the mid-Atlantic states after the American Revolution, the founder principle suggests that the degree of further dialect contact and leveling would have been minimal.

In contrast, at the time of the American Revolution, the lands of western Quebec had no substantial English-speaking population. Since the Loyalist arrivals to this region would have come primarily from the western parts of New England and the inland parts of New York and Pennsylvania, the initial input to (Upper) Canada would have consisted in a mixture of American dialects from these different regions. Further mixing would have taken place with ongoing American input in the form of the late Loyalists. This overwhelmingly American source for the initial English-speaking population to Canada led Morton Bloomfield (1948/1975: 6) to formulate a *Loyalist origins theory*, arguing that Canadian English is "basically eighteenth century American English modified by other influences".

After the War of 1812, with further American immigration largely cut off, the large-scale immigration from different parts of the British Isles would have overwhelmed the smaller existing population. Mark Orkin (1970) presents evidence that a wide variety of British accents could be heard in Canada during the 19th century. This period must have featured another stage of dialect leveling, between the American dialect(s) already spoken in Canada and the incoming mix of British dialects, most of them from Ireland, Scotland and northern England. This British influence led to a second theory about the origins of Canadian English, first promoted by Matthew Scargill (1957/1975), who argued that the British-dialect input might have overpowered the founder effect of the Loyalist population. More recently, Charles Boberg (2004b: 355) has taken a more nuanced position, characterizing Canadian English as a "standard Southern British superstratum . . . imposed on a North American variety". Similarly, Peter Trudgill (2006: 272) views Canadian English as "a mixed dialect par excellence".

The 19th century was also a period in which exonormative forces competed in the stabilization of Canadian English. The founding population spoke American varieties of English but were flooded by immigrants speaking an array of British and Irish varieties. In addition, British North America officially looked to the mother country and metropole for linguistic standards, but geographically (and perhaps culturally) the emerging American standard was much closer. Spelling reforms proposed by Noah Webster in his 1828 dictionary had been widely adopted in the United States to symbolize growing

American linguistic autonomy and nationalism, and American schoolbooks and teachers were much more plentiful in Upper Canada than were their British counterparts. J.K. Chambers (1993) presents evidence from this period showing that educated British English was the object of overt prestige and that local (American) ways of speech were viewed as inferior. However, it may be argued that it is precisely this mixed heritage that was crucial in developing an English Canadian identity. In 1844, John Robert Godley remarked that a national character was forming, distinctive from both American and British, and it is in 1857 that the term "Canadian English" was first used (by the Reverend Geikie, although in a pejorative sense).

By the end of the 19th century we start to see the beginnings of "standard" Canadian English as we know it today, one that is characterized by the absence of regional variation (at least for the thousands of miles between the Ottawa River and Vancouver Island). This homogeneity may stem from two factors: the rapid settlement of the west, which was not opened up for large-scale population until its acquisition after Confederation, and the fact that most of this settlement took place from or through Ontario. Despite the increase in immigrants of central and eastern European background, their children and grandchildren would have tended to shift to English, and the model for that English had already been established in eastern Canada.

During the 20th century, with increasing political autonomy and its external symbols (Canadian citizenship, a Canadian flag, a national anthem) came increasing concern about documenting and codifying Canadian English. The formation of English Canadian identity came with a rejection of American standards and what J.K. Chambers (1998b) has called a "rabid nationalism". As the 20th century progressed and the immigration patterns of Canada's population changed, Canada began to redefine itself as an immigration nation, embracing official bilingualism multiculturalism, as well as *de facto* multilingualism.

A major consequence of the changing patterns of Canadian immigration has been a change in the ethnic and linguistic nature of the urban landscape. Unlike the immigrants who arrived in the late 19th and early 20th centuries to settle the west, late-20th century immigrants have tended to settle in the largest cities: Toronto, Montreal and Vancouver. These more recent immigrants have also come from a wider array of ethnic and linguistic backgrounds than in the past. Although they and their descendants have shifted to English at varying rates, the appearance of urban forms of Canadian English that differentiate speakers according to their ethnic background has been noted. These newer forms of Canadian English raise interesting questions. Do they ultimately derive from transfer from the languages that the immigrant parents and grandparents brought with them (Chambers 1998b)? Will they persist, and will they affect the future shape of Canadian English? We will explore this question in Chapter 7.

SUMMARY

This chapter provided an account of the language-external history that led to the origins and development of English in Canada. We began by outlining the origins and spread of English from Britain to its current status as a worldwide lingua franca, invoking Kachru's concept of World English as a set of concentric circles characterized by the degree to which English is a native language. In order to understand why Canadian English has its current shape, we considered several theories of new-dialect formation. Processes of language transmission and diffusion, founder effects, dialect mixing and language contact can be invoked to understand the similarities and differences between varieties of English.

Having outlined general principles of new-dialect formation, we then outlined a history of the English-speaking people in Canada, beginning with the settlement of Newfoundland and the movement of American Loyalists into what had been a predominantly French-speaking colony. After the War of 1812, the Loyalists were overwhelmed by immigration from the British Isles. Throughout the 19th and early 20th centuries, immigration was opened to western and eastern Europe, with a further opening of immigration throughout the 20th century, leading to profound changes in the ethnic composition of English-speaking Canada by the beginning of the 21st century.

We concluded with some consideration of how these historical, social and demographic forces can be applied to the theories of new-dialect formation to better understand why the linguistic features discussed in the following chapters have the shape that they do. Changes in the ethnolinguistic composition of the English-speaking population of Canada, especially in its largest cities, have been argued to have consequences for the future of Canadian English, a question we will explore in Chapter 7.

4

Lexical Variation

4.0 INTRODUCTION

The previous chapter focused on the language-external considerations that led to the origins and development of Canadian English. We began by looking at how English spread around the world and the principles involved in the formation of new dialects before outlining the historical events that led to the establishment of the English-speaking communities in Canada and then using the principles of new dialect formation to explain the shape that the dialects spoken in these communities have taken. We also considered the role that ideology and language attitudes played in the formation of new norms and standards.

In this and in the next few chapters, we focus on the linguistic characteristics of Canadian English, although we will sometimes need to appeal to language-external considerations to explain the development of these features. Each chapter deals with a different component of the linguistic system: words (lexical features), sounds (phonetic and phonological features) and grammar (morphological, syntactic, semantic and pragmatic features).

This chapter focuses on the lexical features of Canadian English, not only how the vocabulary of Canadian English differs from that of other dialects, but also how Canadian English varies from region to region. I begin by defining what we mean by basic concepts such as *word* and *lexicon*, and I distinguish these concepts from the more commonly understood terms, such as dictionaries. In order to understand the lexical features of Canadian English, it is necessary to first outline the regional structure of the English lexicon, distinguishing between the common lexical heritage shared by all English dialects (which results from the processes of transmission and diffusion discussed in the previous chapter) and dialectal innovation through processes such as borrowing from other languages, coining new words and developing new meanings for old words. This discussion leads to a comparison of the lexical features of North American English with those of other dialects, the lexical features that distinguish Canadian English from American English and regional distinctions within Canadian English. In each of these sections, in addition to using the results of dialect surveys conducted in North America, I will also briefly discuss dictionaries of Canadian English and regional dictionaries.

4.1 LEXICON VS. DICTIONARY

Words are the most noticeable part of language. When people talk about language, they tend to focus on words. Public discussions about language in the media are often concerned with figuring out the "correct" meaning, spelling or usage of particular words. But what is a word? This question might seem silly—English speakers have an intuitive notion of how to recognize words (some might say that they're separated by a space, but this is a convention of writing—we don't separate each word when speaking). However, as we saw in the previous chapter, dialect is also an intuitive notion that becomes problematic once we examine it more closely.

We could define a word as a pairing of sound and meaning. However, as we saw in Chapter 2, words can be broken down into smaller units (morphemes) that also link sound and meaning. One difference between words and morphemes is that words can stand on their own, while morphemes may or may not (i.e. a word necessarily consists of at least one morpheme, but a single morpheme is not necessarily a word). We could then define a word as the smallest pairing of sound and meaning that can stand on its own.

As I mentioned in Chapter 2, Ferdinand de Saussure identified the link between sound and meaning in language as *arbitrary*: there's no reason why a particular string of sounds should correspond to a particular meaning. This is one of the key ways in which languages differ from each other, and a large part of learning a language (whether it's your first, second or fifth language) is memorizing the meanings of different strings of sounds. But if the link between sound and meaning is arbitrary, how do we know what the link is? Saussure also pointed out that sound–meaning correspondences are *conventional*: all speakers of a language agree on the meaning of each string of sounds. However, I should point out that the sound–meaning link is not *completely* conventional. Speakers of the same language will often differ on the meaning of a particular word. New words can also be added to a language, and the meaning of words can change, sometimes in quite drastic ways (as any modern English speaker who has read Shakespeare or Chaucer may have noticed).

If part of learning a language is memorizing all the sound–meaning correspondences, part of the linguistic system must involve storing this information. Although there is some disagreement about the exact shape and content of each speaker's lexical storage (the **mental lexicon**), most linguists would agree that each word or morpheme (or **lexeme**, to use a more general term) *minimally* includes all information that is not predictable from other, more productive processes. So, the entry for each lexeme should not only include its phonological form and its meaning, but also its syntactic category (noun, verb, adjective and so on) and any of its irregularities (such as irregular or suppletive past tense or plural forms).

So far we have been talking about the mental lexicon of individual speakers, but what does it mean to talk about the *English* lexicon? Since it's unlikely that any English speaker knows *every* English word, the English lexicon must be bigger than the mental lexicon of the individual speaker. How do we reconcile these two views? Rather than thinking of a lexicon as a well-defined, self-contained object, it might be better to think of it as a network: some (most?) lexemes are shared by all speakers (basic vocabulary), but some speakers, such as those in different geographical regions or in specialized fields of work, know lexemes that are unfamiliar to other speakers or use lexemes with slightly different meanings. Also, since it is easy for speakers to learn new words (either explicitly or by inferring the meaning of a word from its usage in context), an individual's mental lexicon can change across their lifespan. This view of the lexicon not only allows us to account for regional differences in vocabulary, but it also helps to explain how words change.

Linguists use the term *lexicon* to refer to the stored words of the English language, but most English speakers are probably more accustomed to thinking of dictionaries as the repository of English words. However, the respect for the authority of dictionaries is a consequence of recent traditions of widespread literacy and prescriptivism in European societies over the last few centuries. Dictionaries are concerned with considerations of sound (pronunciation) and meaning, but they also address questions of writing and spelling (**orthography**) that are not relevant to the spoken language. Words existed long before writing was invented, and written language existed for a long time before anyone felt the need to list all the words in their language. The earliest dictionaries that we know of had quite different purposes than those that we use nowadays. They consisted of lists of corresponding words in different languages to be used for translation or administration in societies where many languages were spoken. The first English dictionaries that appeared in the 16th and 17th centuries were intended as an aid to translation from other languages, and the first known monolingual English dictionary (Robert Cawdrey's [1604] *A Table Alphabeticall*) only included "difficult" words that would have been unfamiliar or obscure to most readers.

The type of dictionary that we are most familiar with today, which aims to provide a comprehensive list of words and includes detailed information about meanings, spellings and sometimes the origins and histories of words (**etymology**) only appeared in the 18th century, when the modern profession of dictionary-making, or **lexicography**, began. Samuel Johnson's (1755) *A Dictionary of the English Language* was the first attempt to be comprehensive, as well as to provide a guide to pronunciation and meaning. Noah Webster's (1828) *An American Dictionary of the English Language,* which not only included words not used in Britain but also initiated or promoted a number of spelling reforms that are used in American English until this day, was, in part, a patriotic attempt to differentiate American English from its British origins. Probably the most comprehensive English dictionary is the *Oxford English Dictionary* (OED), which was begun in 1884 under the editorship of James Murray, and the first edition of which was not completed until 1928. The OED was established on "historical principles", in which each word is traced to its first appearance in print. Nowadays there are updated versions of Webster's dictionary and the OED, as well as numerous other English dictionaries, not only those that aim to be comprehensive, but also those for regional, national or specialized vocabulary.

Dictionaries have two different purposes. Johnson's and Webster's dictionaries were intended, in part, as normative or **prescriptive** dictionaries, to instruct readers in the *correct* meaning, spelling and usage of words, and to prevent the language from changing. Part of the socialization involved in education in the English-speaking world includes an inculcation of a prescriptivist ideology of language, with an appeal to dictionaries as arbiters of correctness. More recently, dictionaries have taken on a **descriptive** purpose, documenting the different pronunciations, spellings, meanings and usages of each word without indicating correctness. While their purpose is not to prescribe standards, some descriptive dictionaries provide guidelines for accepted usage.

4.2 CANADIANISMS

In the previous section, I suggested that the English lexicon is best viewed as a network of individual mental lexicons. If we look at this network regionally, all varieties of English share a common core vocabulary but differ from each other because of innovations that have taken place in each variety since their divergence from each other. The regional structure of the English lexicon can be visualized as in Figure 4.1.

At the highest level, all varieties of English share lexemes inherited from their common origin, as a result of the process of language transmission that we discussed in the previous chapter (as indicated by the solid lines). These lexemes include the basic vocabulary of English that developed out of its Anglo-Saxon roots and was augmented by influence and borrowing from French and Scandinavian languages. In the process of spreading through the world, different regional varieties developed and innovated in different ways.

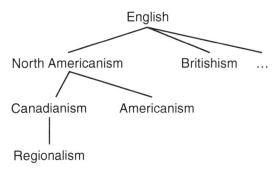

FIGURE 4.1 Intervarietal structure of the English lexicon

The establishment of the English-speaking communities outside of Britain took place at a time when intercontinental travel and communication were very slow. For example, in the 17th century it could take up to two months to travel just from Britain to the east coast of North America, and the First Fleet took eight months to travel to Australia in 1787–88. In the absence of tele-communication (telegraphs, telephones, radio and so on), news only travels as quickly as the fastest ship. These distances meant that the regular interaction among speakers needed to maintain community speech conventions became weakened, and different varieties of English became free to innovate. Given the encounters with new cultures and unknown flora and fauna, an obvious source of new words in new English dialects was the wholesale importation from other languages, or **lexical borrowing**. While English already had a long history of borrowing—from Latin, French and the Scandinavian languages— English speakers in each of the new communities were exposed to different lan-guages, leading to new English words such as *boss, cookie, canoe* and *boomerang* (see below). New words are also coined by combining words or morphemes that already exist in the language (through affixation and compounding), such as *skyscraper* or *telephone*. Words are sometimes invented from scratch (**neolo-gisms**), such as *blurb* and *xerox*. Such innovations led to increasing differences in the lexicons of the new varieties of English that developed in the 17th to 19th centuries and gave rise to lexical **regionalisms** (Americanisms, Canadi-anisms, Australianisms and so on).

Yet words are easily acquired. As transportation and communication within the English-speaking world became faster, there was increasing contact between English varieties. Through the process of diffusion discussed in the preceding chapter, lexical innovations in one variety could spread to another, potentially obscuring regional differences. So unless we know the history of a particular word, it may be difficult to determine its origin.

These considerations mean that deciding whether a particular English word should be considered a regionalism may be made in several ways. First, a word may be considered a regionalism if it *originated* in a particular region, regardless of whether it is now used elsewhere. The word *boomerang* clearly originated in Australia (borrowed from aboriginal languages spoken in New South Wales), yet most English speakers know this word. Second, a word may be considered a regionalism if it has *unique occurrence* in a particular region, even if it originated elsewhere. For example, the Canadian English word *riding* ("a voting district") originated in Britain but is no longer used there. Third, a word may be considered a regionalism if it has a *unique meaning* in one region. For example, among the meanings of *root* in Australian English is a slang term for "copulate", a meaning it does not have in other English varieties. Finally, we can appeal to considerations of frequency: different words for the same thing coexist in many English-speaking communities, but if a word is more frequent in a particular region, it may be considered a regionalism (as we will see below).

As Figure 4.1 shows, regionalisms are not the same as national boundaries. Canadian and American English share a number of terms that can be classed as **North Americanisms**, as they are either only used in North America or are used with meanings that differ from other varieties of English. Canadians and Americans put *gas* rather than *petrol* in their cars, they drive a *truck* rather than a *lorry* and parents push their baby in a *carriage* rather than in a *pram*. The words *yard* and *garden* have opposite meanings in North America and Britain: in Britain, a garden is larger than a yard, but in North America the reverse is true. In North America, to be *pissed* (or *pissed off*) means to be angry, while in Britain it means to be drunk. To *knock up* someone in North America is to get her pregnant, while in Britain it means to wake someone up.

Both American and Canadian English feature words originally borrowed from other languages, such as *boss* and *cookie* from Dutch and *canoe* from Carib via Spanish. Canadian English has borrowed further from the languages spoken by other people who played a major role in founding and settling the country. From French come *aboiteau* (an Acadian term referring to a technique for farming on marshland), *coureur de bois* (a fur trapper or trader), *dépanneur* (or *dep*, a convenience store) and *touque*, a knitted hat. From the First Nations languages come *moccasin* (a leather shoe) from Algonquian, *pemmican* (a mixture of fat, berries and meat) from Cree and *kayak* (a small covered boat propelled with a paddle) from Inuktitut.

Canadian English also features a number of neologisms, words either blended from other elements or invented from scratch. For example, a native speaker of English is referred to as an *anglophone* and a native French speaker as a *francophone*, while someone whose first language is something other than French or English is an *allophone*. A Canadian is often referred to by the term *Canuck*, the origin of which is unclear, but it seems to have originally been an American term used to refer to a French Canadian. As in other English-speaking political contexts, members of the Conservative party are referred to as *Tories*, but in Canada members of the Liberal parties are *Grits*. Canadian meteorologists use the term *humidex* (a blend of *humidity* and *index*) to describe how hot it feels once you factor the humidity into the heat. More recent neologisms include *loonie*, an informal term for the one-dollar coin introduced in 1987 (because of the loon depicted on the tail side of the coin) and *toonie*, a blend of *two* and *loonie*, which refers to the two-dollar coin introduced in 1996. Another recent neologism is *grow op* (or *grow-op*), a clipping of *grow opportunity* (or *grow operation*), which refers to an illegal marijuana cultivation operation.

A number of words that occur elsewhere in the English-speaking world have distinctive usages in Canadian English. A voting district is referred to as a *riding*, a Canadian will ask to use the *washroom* rather than the *restroom*, a single-room apartment is referred to as a *bachelor apartment*, First Nations people may live on an Indian *reserve*, Canadians use a *serviette* rather than a *napkin*, they eat with *cutlery* rather than *utensils* and they will tend to stand in a *line up* rather than a *line* or a *queue*. One of the most distinctive unique usages in Canadian English is the term *chesterfield*, which refers to a piece of furniture that is otherwise called a *couch* or *sofa*.

Perhaps because of the extent to which English Canada looked toward foreign standards of linguistic behaviour—British or American—dictionaries of Canadian English are relatively recent. As with the earliest English dictionaries, Canadian English was first recognized as a separate variety in a bilingual dictionary, *Nugent's Up-to-Date English-French and French-English Dictionary*, published in 1905 by Sylva Clapin, who had already published *A New Dictionary of American-isms: Being a Glossary of Words Supposed to be Peculiar to the United States and the Dominion of Canada* (1902). Throughout the 20th century there were a number of dictionaries produced for the Canadian market, but they tended to be specialized or reduced versions of American dictionaries, such as the *Winston Simplified Dictionary for Canadian Schools* (Brown and Alexander 1937), based on the American *Winston Simplified Dictionary* (1919). The first stand-alone monolingual dictionary of Canadian English was John Sandilands's (1912) *Western Canadian Dictionary and Phrase Book*, although it was primarily intended as a guide for new arrivals to the western territories to understand some of the local turns of phrase. However, it has been pointed out that the aim of this dictionary was not to provide a comprehensive account of western Canadian English, and that many of the words and phrases recorded by Sandilands were not unique to Canadian English but were also used in the United States.

It was not until the foundation of the Canadian Linguistic Association in 1954 that serious consideration was given to developing a comprehensive dictionary of Canadian English on the same principles of the OED. The first volume of the *Dictionary of Canadian English* (Avis 1962) was followed by the more detailed *Dictionary of Canadianisms on Historical Principles* (Avis 1967).

In the 1990s, other dictionaries of Canadian English appeared, such as the *ITP Nelson Canadian Dictionary of the English Language* (ITP Nelson 1996) and the *Canadian Oxford Dictionary* (Barber 1998), along with regional dictionaries of Newfoundland English (Story, Kirwin and Widdowson 1982) and Prince Edward Island English (Pratt 1988).

Apart from regionalisms, another concern of Canadian English lexicography is the issue of orthography, or spelling. Up until the 18th century there was a great deal of variation in English spelling, with writers (and, later, printers) spelling words according to how they themselves pronounced them and/or introducing their own idiosyncrasies into their spelling. One of the goals of Johnson's dictionary was to standardize spelling so that anyone could recognize a word on the basis of its spelling no matter how they pronounced it. As noted in Chapter 3, although Canada was a British colony, its geographic proximity to the United States meant that schoolteachers and the textbooks they used tended to be American more than British. As a result, Canadian English has always been torn between the British spelling standards of its former mother country and the American spelling standards of its nearer and larger neighbour. This conflict has resulted in a compromise situation in which a great deal of variation is tolerated. However, for some words there is a clear preference for British spelling (*harbour* instead of *harbor*, *centre* instead of *center*, *cheque* instead of *check*) and for others for American spelling (*curb* for *kerb*, *tire* for *tyre*, *jail* for *gaol*).

4.3 STUDYING REGIONAL VARIATION

While *lexicography* seeks to collect and define all the words of a language, the goal of *dialectology* is to understand how language differs from place to place. The interest in dialect differences developed during the 18th and 19th centuries, when processes of state formation and centralization, along with codification and standardization of language, led to concerns that regional dialects needed to be documented before they disappeared. This concern for dialect preservation was part of the Romantic movement of the same period, which viewed the culture and language of the countryside as embodying the national character.

Dialectology differs from lexicography not only in its goals but also in its methods of data collection. Rather than documenting the lexicon through written documents, dialectology is concerned with collecting words as they are actually used by speakers of the language. To this end, dialectology tends to make use of techniques of elicitation. In order to ensure that the results for each speaker will be comparable, dialectologists have tended to make use of dialect questionnaires that contain a list of questions concerning words of specific interest.

Dialect surveys have made use of different types of questions, depending on the kind of data they want to elicit. Questions can be open ended, such as "What do you call the shoes you wear to play sports?" (or "What do you call this?" with a picture of the shoe), or they can be closed, so that the respondent has to choose from a list, such as: "(a) running shoes, (b) runners, (c) sneakers".

Data can also be elicited in different ways depending on the type of data required as well as the degree of literacy of the respondents. In the earliest dialect survey (1876–86), Georg Wenker mailed a questionnaire containing questions about local dialect forms to schoolmasters at thousands of locations around Germany. In Jules Gilliéron's dialect survey of France (1896–1900), his fieldworker Edmond Edmont traveled the country administering the questionnaire and recording responses. In addition to postal surveys and fieldwork surveys, recent dialect surveys have made use of the telephone and the Internet to administer questionnaires to potential respondents.

Since the goal of dialectology is to understand regional differences in language, the responses to each question are normally recorded by indicating the variant used and the location of the response on a map. When multiple responses are recorded, we begin to see patterns of regional distribution. Figure 4.2 shows a hypothetical result from a dialect survey, distinguishing between two lexical variants (indicated by triangles and circles). If we have a good representation of locations, we can draw an **isogloss** on the map, a line that separates two geographic regions in which different variants are used.

Normally we want to take into consideration more than one isogloss, to look for places where isoglosses coincide. Bundling of isoglosses gives us confidence in claiming the existence of a **dialect area**.

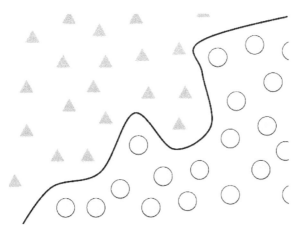

FIGURE 4.2 Hypothetical dialect map with an isogloss separating two regions in which different variants (indicated with triangles and circles) are used

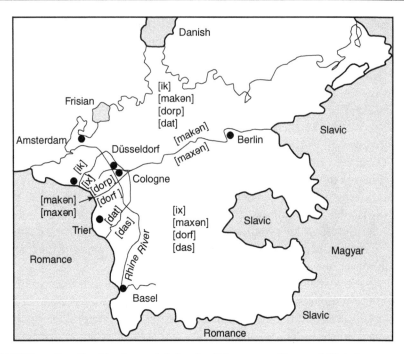

FIGURE 4.3 Bundle of isoglosses defining the dialect areas of Low and High German
Source: Adapted from Bloomfield 1933/84: 344.

Figure 4.3 shows a famous bundle of isoglosses that cuts across northern Germany. To the north, speakers pronounce the words *ich* ("I"), *machen* ("make", "do"), *Dorf* ("village") and *das* ("the [neuter]") as [ik], [makən], [dorp] and [dat], respectively (with stops), while to the south, these words are pronounced as [ix], [maxən], [dorf] and [das] (with fricatives). Although as they approach the river Rhine these isoglosses begin to spread out (the so-called "Rhenish fan"), the bundling of these isoglosses over most of their length is taken to define the boundary between northern (Low) German and southern (High) German.

Large-scale surveys of North American English were undertaken in the first half of the 20th century, but their treatment of Canadian English was mainly incidental. The first *Survey of Canadian English* (another goal at the foundation of the Canadian Linguistic Association) was only published in 1972 (Scargill and Warkentyne 1972), followed by regional surveys in locales such as Vancouver (Gregg 1992) and Ottawa (Woods 1979). These surveys revealed regional differences in the choice of Canadianisms as well as a tendency for younger speakers to increase their use of Americanisms.

In contrast with traditional dialect geography, which is concerned with mapping regional variation, *dialect topography* (Chambers 1998a) also takes

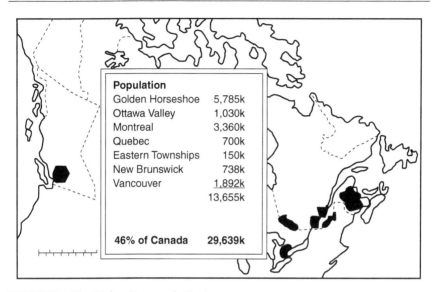

Population	
Golden Horseshoe	5,785k
Ottawa Valley	1,030k
Montreal	3,360k
Quebec	700k
Eastern Townships	150k
New Brunswick	738k
Vancouver	1,892k
	13,655k
46% of Canada	**29,639k**

FIGURE 4.4 The Dialect Topography Project

Source: Figure 1, Chambers 2007: 29.

into account the distribution of lexical variants within each region according to social characteristics. For example, by incorporating speaker age as a factor, we can infer the existence of ongoing lexical change.

J. K. Chambers's *Dialect Topography Project*, conducted in the 1990s, covered seven English-speaking regions of Canada, shown in Figure 4.4: the "Golden Horseshoe" (the western end of Lake Ontario, stretching from Toronto's eastern suburbs to the Niagara region), the Ottawa Valley, Montreal, Quebec City, the Eastern Townships, New Brunswick and (on the west coast) Vancouver. Using a questionnaire (first distributed in hard copy by mail, later collected online), he asked 11 personal data questions and 76 questions about linguistic variables, with open-ended responses. For example, Figure 4.5 shows the regional distribution of words for athletic footwear (*sneakers, running shoes* and *runners*) across the different English-speaking regions of Canada, as well as two border regions in New York State. Although all three terms can be found in each region of Canada, and two can be found in at least one of the US regions, there is a clear preference for one variant (*running shoes*) across all regions of Canada and for another (*sneakers*) in both US regions. So we are justified in viewing *running shoes* as a Canadianism.

Chambers's survey also asked respondents questions about their social characteristics. In Figure 4.6, which shows the distribution by both region and age for the use of *snuck* (vs. *sneaked*) as a past tense of the verb *sneak*,

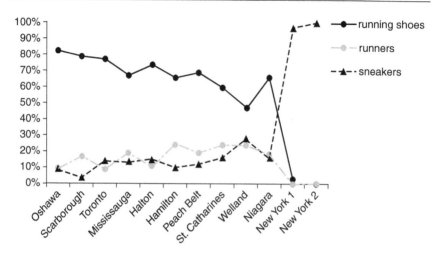

FIGURE 4.5 Regional distribution of terms for athletic footwear

Source: Figure 3, Chambers 2000: 187.

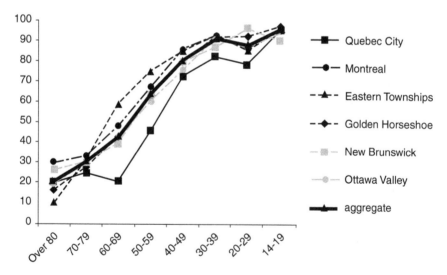

FIGURE 4.6 Distribution of past-tense *snuck* (vs. *sneaked*) by age and region

Source: Figure 2, Chambers 2007: 31.

there is a clear correlation between the use of this variant and the respondent's age: the younger the respondent, the more likely they are to prefer *snuck*. This correlation, which holds regardless of region, suggests that a change has taken place in Canadian English for this lexical item within the last few generations.

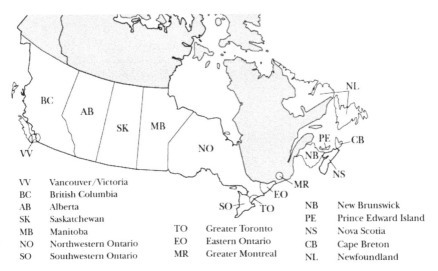

VV   Vancouver/Victoria
BC   British Columbia
AB   Alberta
SK   Saskatchewan
MB   Manitoba   TO   Greater Toronto   NS   Nova Scotia
NO   Northwestern Ontario   EO   Eastern Ontario   CB   Cape Breton
SO   Southwestern Ontario   MR   Greater Montreal   NL   Newfoundland

NB   New Brunswick
PE   Prince Edward Island

FIGURE 4.7 Canadian regions of the North American Regional Vocabulary Survey (NARVS)

Source: Boberg 2005.

Charles Boberg's (2005) more recent *North American Regional Vocabulary Survey* (NARVS) collected responses from a written questionnaire consisting of 53 questions covering most of the English-speaking regions of Canada. In addition to each of the nine provinces other than Quebec, the major metropolitan areas (Vancouver-Victoria, Toronto and Montreal) were considered separately, and, as the largest and most populous province, Ontario was divided into northern, eastern and southern regions (see Figure 4.7).

Rather than determining isoglosses on the basis of individual lexical variants, Boberg (2005) uses two aggregate measurements of differences between regions: *net variation*, which sums all the differences in percentages for each variant between each region, and *major isoglosses*, which takes as meaningful any difference of 50% or more in percentage for each variable between regions. Table 4.1 shows a comparison of each region with its immediate neighbour, in terms of both net variation and major isoglosses, for 44 lexical variables in NARVS. The greatest distinction is between Montreal (MR) and its neighbours: not only does it feature the highest net variation (62–54%) but also the most major isoglosses (17–9). The next highest distinction is between Newfoundland (NL) and its immediate neighbours (45–44% net variation and 8–5 major isoglosses). The remaining differences between regions begin to show some disagreement between net variation and major isoglosses, but there do seem to be differences that suggest a western dialect region (British Columbia, Alberta, Saskatchewan and Manitoba) and a Maritime dialect region (New Brunswick, Nova Scotia and Prince Edward Island), with Ontario forming its own dialect region. Table 4.2 provides the top 10 words that differentiate between these regions (note that the numbers in Table 4.2

TABLE 4.1

Regional Lexical Differences Within Canada

Division	Net Variation	Sig. less than	Division	Major Isoglosses
MR-NB	62%	–	MR-NB	17
EO-MR	54%	–	EO-MR	9
NS-NL	45%	MR-NB	NS-NL	8
CB-NL	44%	MR-NB	CB-NL	5
PE-NS	40%	EO-MR	NO-SO	5
MB-NO	39%	EO-MR	NB-PE	3
NB-PE	37%	EO-MR	PE-NS	2
SK-MB	37%	EO-MR	MB-NO	2
BC-AB	33%	PE-NS	SK-MB	1
SO-TO	32%	PE-NS	AB-SK	1
NS-CB	31%	MB-NO	BC-AB	0
NO-SO	30%	MB-NO	VV-BC	0
VV-BC	29%	SK-MB	NS-CB	0
TO-EO	28%	SK-MB	TO-EO	0
NB-NS	27%	BC-AB	NB-NS	0
AB-SK	26%	SO-TO	SO-TO	0

Source: Table 2, Boberg 2005: 35

TABLE 4.2

Top 10 Lexical Regional Differences Within Canada

Lexical Variable	Net Variation	Isoglosses
cabin/cottage/chalet	1212%	6
parking garage/parkade	1107%	3
pizza with all the toppings	1062%	5
internship/stage	1045%	
convenience/corner store/dépanneur	1020%	3
see-saw/teeter-totter	996%	4
notebook/scribbler	960%	5
backpack/bookbag/schoolbag	917%	3
carbonated beverage	908%	4
burger with all the toppings	852%	3

Source: Table 3, Boberg 2005: 41

indicate the sum of net variation across all regions for the variants of each lexical variable, so are not percentages in the strict sense). Many of these terms are unique to Montreal and clearly represent influence from French: *chalet, pizza all-dressed, stage* (with French pronunciation), *dépanneur* and *soft drink*. However, several terms serve to distinguish other regions, with *cabin* preferred in the west and New-foundland, *parkade* preferred in the west and *scribbler* preferred in the Maritimes.

In addition to regional variation within Canada, NARVS also included responses from neighbouring American regions in order to investigate differences between American English and Canadian English vocabulary. Table 4.3 shows the top five lexical items that differentiate responses in the United States and in Canada. Notice that these lexical items are completely different from those in Table 4.2, demonstrating the difference between Americanisms, Canadianisms and regionalisms within Canada.

Finally, we might ask whether Canadian English vocabulary is becoming more American. In Figures 4.8 and 4.9, the two measures of distance (net

TABLE 4.3

Top Five Lexical Items Distinguishing American English and Canadian English

American Variant		Canadian Variant	
first grade	98%	grade one	87%
candy bar	84%	chocolate bar	87%
faucet	91%	tap	75%
zee	98%	zed	70%
studio apartment	62%	bachelor apartment	62%

Source: Table 5, Boberg 2005: 46

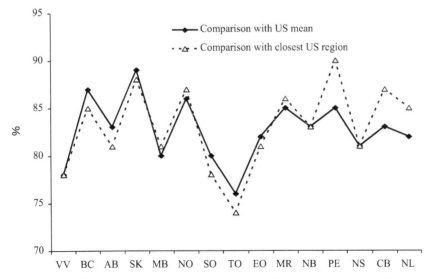

FIGURE 4.8 Differences in net lexical variation between Canada and the United States
Source: Adapted from Table 7, Boberg 2005: 51.

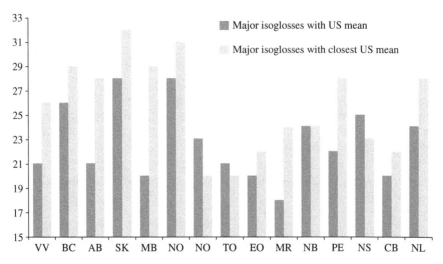

FIGURE 4.9 Differences in major lexical isoglosses between Canada and the United States
Source: Adapted from Table 8, Boberg 2005: 52.

variation and major isoglosses) are compared for each region of Canadian English to the overall mean for the US responses, and for the closest US region for each Canadian region. No Canadian region stands out as being more "American" than any other region by either measure, though the differences seem to be smallest for the largest cities (Toronto and Vancouver), which might suggest a relationship between urban centres and (the perception of) Americanization.

SUMMARY

This chapter focused on variation in the lexicon of Canadian English, not only its differences from other varieties of English but also regional differences within Canada. We began by defining basic linguistic concepts such as "lexeme" and "lexicon", distinguishing them from the ordinary understanding of word and dictionary. We can think of the English lexicon as a network of lexicons distinguished on the one hand by elements of common heritage and on the other by regional differences that result from processes of borrowing, innovation and semantic shift. Lexicography concerns the description of lexicons through dictionaries, either prescriptive or descriptive, while dialect surveys concern the geographic distribution of linguistic variation and the development of dialect maps. An additional dimension to the study of lexical variation is provided by dialect topography, which concerns not only geographic distribution but also the social factors that condition lexical choice.

5

Phonetic and Phonological Variation

5.1 INTRODUCTION

In the previous chapter, we discussed the lexical features of Canadian English, examining their similarities with those of other varieties of English due to their common inheritance through processes such as transmission and diffusion, as well as dialectal differences and regionalisms that arose from different strategies of lexical innovation, such as borrowing, semantic shift and neologism.

In this chapter, we turn to the sound system of Canadian English; that is, the organization of the phonological system into phonemic distinctions and their phonetic realizations. As we did with lexical features, we can explain some of the phonological and phonetic similarities of Canadian English with other varieties of English through the common inheritance from Britain and from the Loyalist Americans. However, lexical features and phonological features differ in a couple of respects. While words are easily acquired throughout life and easily spread from variety to variety through diffusion, phonemes and their phonetic realization are more resistant to change across the lifespan of an individual and are much harder to acquire in adulthood (as anyone who has tried to learn another language as an adult knows). In addition, while lexical borrowing and innovation are common processes, the borrowing and innovation of phonological distinctions or phonetic realizations are much rarer. Because of these differences between lexical and phonological features, any divergence in the phonological system between Canadian English and other varieties of English requires recourse to explanations other than innovation and borrowing.

When people speak of the Canadian "accent", they often note that it is remarkably homogeneous across the country, without the sharp regional differences that characterize the English spoken in Britain, or even in the United States. However, this generalization really only applies to the Canadian English that is spoken in the area stretching from eastern Ontario to Vancouver Island in the west. In this chapter, I will refer to this variety as *General Canadian English* (GCE). This variety encompasses most of the country and the majority of its English-speaking population, but there are audible differences between GCE and the varieties spoken in other regions, such as the province of Quebec (primarily Montreal, though there are other English-speaking communities throughout the province), the Maritime provinces (Nova Scotia, New Brunswick and Prince Edward Island) and Newfoundland. As we will see, there may also be regional differences within GCE that are not easily audible but may be revealed through more detailed phonetic and sociolinguistic analysis.

In this chapter, I will begin by discussing the phonological and phonetic features of GCE, focusing on those consonant and vowel features that distinguish the Canadian English accent from other English accents. I will discuss some of the issues involved in studying regional variation in phonology and phonetics (and how they differ from studying lexical variation) before I consider regional variation in Canadian English sound systems.

5.2 PHONOLOGICAL FEATURES OF GENERAL CANADIAN ENGLISH

5.2.1 Consonants

Varieties of English do not greatly differ from each other in their inventory of consonant phonemes, but they do sometimes differ in the way these phonemes are realized phonetically. As Table 5.1 shows, the phonemic inventory of consonants for GCE is largely the same as that of other varieties of English, but some of these phonemes exhibit additional phonetic variation according to social and stylistic considerations. The interdental consonants, as in *thing* and *there*, are normally realized as the voiced and voiceless fricatives [θ] and [ð], respectively. The voiced phoneme /ð/ sometimes occurs as a stopped [d] in casual contexts ("th-stopping"), especially in function words like *the*, and more commonly in the speech of rural or working-class speakers and urban speakers of different ethnic backgrounds. The coronal stops /t/ and /d/ occur as a voiced flap or tap [ɾ] when they are preceded by a stressed vowel and followed by another vowel or a syllabic sonorant ([l̩], [ɹ̩] or [n̩]), as in *potato* [pʰəˈtʰeɪɾoʷ] or *ladder* [ˈlærɾ]. In GCE, as in General American English, /l/ after a vowel or in its syllabic form is realized as a "dark" or velar [ɫ], as opposed to a clear [l], as in *milk* [mɪɫk], and /r/, which is realized as a retroflex approximant [ɹ], is always pronounced after vowels and as a syllabic nucleus, as in *north* [nɔɹθ] and *nurse* [nɹ̩s]. Thus, GCE is a **rhotic** variety of English.

As noted, consonant phonemes exhibit some variation in their phonetic realization. Coronal stops followed by the diphthong [ju], such as *tune* and

TABLE 5.1

Consonant phonemes of General Canadian English

		BILABIAL	LABIO-DENTAL	INTER-DENTAL	ALVEO-LAR	PALATO-ALVEOLAR	PALATAL	VELAR	GLOTTAL
Stop	Voiceless	p			t			k	
	Voiced	b			d			g	
Fricative	Voiceless		f	θ	s				h
	Voiced		v	ð	z				
Affricate	Voiceless					tʃ			
	Voiced					dʒ			
Approximant		(w)			r		j	(w)	
Nasal		m			n			ŋ	
Lateral					l				

dune, are normally palatalized as [tʲuʷn] and [dʲuʷn], but some speakers drop the palatal articulation ("yod-dropping") so that *tune* sounds like [tʰuʷn], or they combine the coronal stop and the palatal into a palato-alveolar affricate ("yod-coalescence"), so that *tune* is pronounced as [tʃuʷn]). While speakers of GCE currently do not distinguish between voiced [w] and voiceless [ʍ] in words such as *what*, it was reported in the past among older speakers (e.g. I heard it in the speech of my maternal grandfather, a Canadian of Irish background who grew up in the Ottawa Valley in the early 20th century). However, Sali Tagliamonte (personal communication) has noted its current use in data she has collected in northern Ontario.

5.2.2 Vowels

Unlike differences in the phonemic organization of consonants, the phonemics of vowel systems serve to distinguish among varieties of English. As we saw in Chapter 2, while the production of consonants is relatively discrete, production of vowels is continuous in two dimensions: height and backness/frontness. In theory, a virtually infinite number of divisions of the vowel space into phonemic distinctions is possible. But the continuous nature of vowel production, in which the space of neighbouring vowels can potentially overlap with each other, is at odds with the phonemic imperative to maximize the distinction between contrastive sounds.

As with consonants, varieties of English may share the same inventory of vowel phonemes but differ in how those phonemes are realized phonetically. For example, the English phoneme /o/ as in *coat* is realized in North American English as [oʷ] but in Australian English as [əʉ]. The vowel phonemes of different varieties may also be distinguished by their *phonemic incidence*, the distribution of allophones according to elements of the linguistic context. For example, some varieties of English make a distinction in low vowels before fricatives and nasals, such that *trap* and *bath* (and *dance*) have different phonetic realizations in British English ([æ] and [ɑː]), but not in North American English.

More crucially, phonemic vowel systems of English varieties are distinguished by their inventories of phonemic contrasts. Because the phonetic realization of a vowel is never exactly the same, it is more accurate to think of vowel phonemes as occupying an area of the vowel space than as discrete points. If the area of one vowel begins to overlap with that of another vowel, two vowel phonemes may end up becoming **merged** as one phoneme. For example, the reason that *meet* and *meat* are spelled differently but pronounced the same is that the Early Modern English /ɛː/ vowel (spelled as *ea*) merged with the /eː/ vowel (spelled as *ee*) (Wells 1982). Alternatively, the area occupied by the other vowel may move away in order to maintain the phonemic contrast, encroaching on the area of another

TABLE 5.2

Phonemic Inventory of Vowels in General Canadian English

	SHORT		LONG	
	FRONT	BACK	FRONT	BACK
HIGH	ɪ	ʊ	i	u
MID	ɛ	ʌ	e	o
LOW	æ			ɑ
DIPHTHONG			ay ɔy	ay

Source: Adapted from Wells 1982

vowel, which itself may move away, and so on, resulting in a **chain shift**. For example, the Great English Vowel Shift, which took place in the 15th and 16th centuries, involved a shift of the long vowels along the path /a:/ → /e:/ → /i:/ → / ay/ (e.g. *mate* to [me:t], *meet* (and *meat*) to [mi:t], *mite* to [mayt], which explains why the English pronunciation of vowel letters is at odds with their pronunciation in other European languages). Less common but also possible is a split of two phonemes, in which different parts of a vowel's area begin to separate until they end up becoming two phonemes. While dialects of English have probably always been characterized by diversity in their phonemic inventory of vowels, the operation of mergers, shifts and splits in the centuries since the spread and diversification of English (see Chapter 3) has acted to reorganize the vowel systems of English varieties in different ways.

In the phonemic vowel inventory of GCE presented in Table 5.2 there are three main features distinguishing it from other varieties of English, one involving a vowel merger, one involving phonemic incidence and another involving a vowel shift.

The Low-Back Merger

Canadian English is distinguished from many other English vowel systems by the complete merger of the low and low-back vowels /ɑ/, /ɒ/ and /ɔ/ (in terms of Wells's [1982] lexical sets, the PALM, LOT and THOUGHT vowels), which are all realized phonetically as [ɑ]. This merger, sometimes referred to as the *cot/caught* merger, seems to be a continuation of the reorganization of the low-back vowels that began in Early Modern English. Another feature of low vowels that helps to distinguish GCE from American English is whether foreign loanwords such as *drama* and *pasta* are adapted to English as either /æ/ or /ɑ/. GCE prefers adaptation to /æ/, such that *pasta* is pronounced as [pʰæstə].

Canadian Raising

Perhaps the most salient feature of GCE is the raising of the onset of the diphthongs /ay/ and /aw/ before voiceless consonants, leading to different pronunciations of the vowels in *prize* [prayz] versus *price* [prəys] and *house (verb)* [hawz] versus *house* (noun) [həws]. (See Figure 2.3 on p. 12.) This difference leads Americans to believe that they're hearing Canadians say *out and about* as *oot and aboot*. This feature of GCE was first identified by Martin Joos in 1942 and was labeled by J.K. Chambers (1973/1975) as *Canadian Raising*. Using the notation of phonological rules prevalent at the time, he formulated the rule of Canadian Raising, as in (5.1).

$$(5.1) \quad \begin{bmatrix} V \\ +\text{tense} \end{bmatrix} \rightarrow \begin{bmatrix} -\text{low} \end{bmatrix} / \_\_ \text{ GLIDE} \begin{bmatrix} C \\ -\text{voice} \end{bmatrix}$$

As Chambers notes, the label "Canadian" is a bit misleading, since raised realizations of these diphthongs occur in some varieties of English in the United States and the British Isles. What may be unique to Canadian English is the phonemic incidence of the raising (only before voiceless consonants), which Peter Trudgill (1986, 2006) argues to have come about as a result of the processes involved in dialect leveling that took place during the development of GCE in Upper Canada in the mid-19th century (see p. 40). As we saw in Chapter 3, the input to this variety included American Loyalist English, in which the onset of the diphthongs was not raised, and other varieties of English in which the onset of the diphthongs was always raised (northern English and Irish and, most notably, Scottish immigrants). Although the Loyalists constituted the founding population of English-speaking Canada, throughout the 19th century their numbers were overwhelmed by British immigration, predominantly from northern Britain and from Ireland. Under Trudgill's account, a situation in which the two variants (raised and nonraised onsets) were originally interpreted as regional became structurally reallocated to different linguistic contexts: raised before voiceless consonants, unraised elsewhere. If Trudgill's account of the origins of Canadian Raising is correct, we should expect to find evidence for its existence by the end of the 19th century. Although we do not of course have recorded data from the time period in which the reallocation would have taken place, we do have indirect evidence. In 1991 Erik Thomas analyzed data collected in the 1940s and 1950s as part of a dialectological survey of the United States that included informants in Ontario who had been born in the late 19th century. Thomas assigned each respondent an index score, with a higher score indicating more raising, and mapped the geographical distribution of the scores for /aw/ and /ay/, as shown in Figures 5.1 and 5.2, respectively. Although

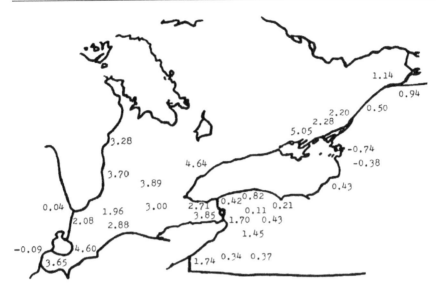

FIGURE 5.1 Regional distribution of /aw/-raising, late 19th century

Source: Map 1, Thomas 1991.

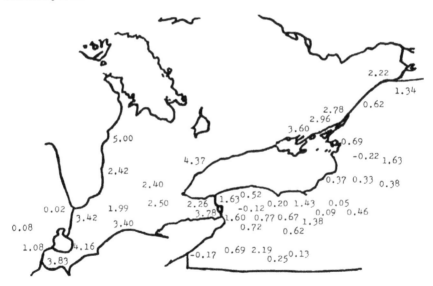

FIGURE 5.2 Regional distribution of /ay/-raising, late 19th century

Source: Map 2, Thomas 1991.

the scores on the Ontario side of the border vary a great deal (between 1.14 for /aw/ in Cornwall to 5.05 for /aw/ in Belleville), they are consistently higher than those on the American side of the border. If we assume that the respondents had acquired their phonological systems in childhood and early adolescence (see Chapter 7), this distribution would suggest that Canadian Raising was already established as a feature of Canadian English around the time of Confederation.

The Canadian Vowel Shift

As noted above, the vowel systems of English varieties that developed as the language spread and diversified over the last few centuries have been distinguished by the different vowel mergers, shifts and splits that have taken place in each. William Labov (1991) has identified three dialects of English based on the mergers and shifts taking place in North American English. The first dialect is undergoing the Northern Cities Shift (NCS), which primarily occurs in northern US cities such as Syracuse, Rochester and Buffalo (New York), Detroit (Michigan) and Chicago (Illinois). The NCS involves the fronting of /a/ to [æ] and the raising of /æ/ to [ɛ], among other components shown in Figure 5.3. The second dialect, which encompasses the southeastern United States, is undergoing the Southern Shift. As shown in Figure 5.4, the Southern Shift involves the merger of the vowels in *pin* and *pen* and the monophthongization of /ay/ to [aː], among other features. Labov characterizes the third dialect, which encompasses the remainder of English-speaking North America, by the absence of vowel shifts.

However, in a 1995 study, Sandra Clarke and her associates provided the first evidence for an ongoing shift in the vowel system of Canadian English,

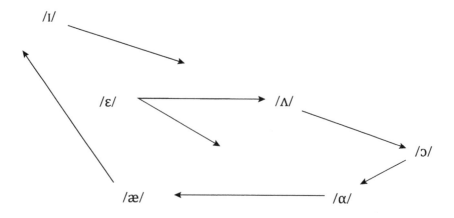

FIGURE 5.3 The Northern Cities Shift

which they called the Canadian Vowel Shift (CVS). As illustrated in Figure 5.5, the CVS involves the retraction and lowering of the front lax vowels /ɪ/, /ɛ/ and /æ/, along with the lowering of /ʌ/ and /ʊ/. Clarke and her associates argue that the CVS is a chain shift, initially triggered by the *cot/caught* merger, which

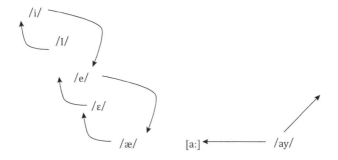

FIGURE 5.4 The Southern Shift

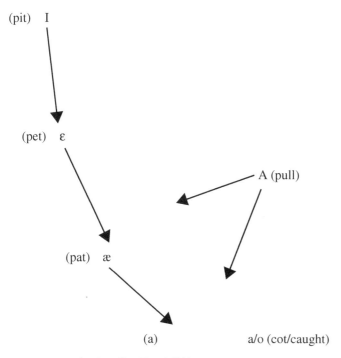

FIGURE 5.5 The Canadian Vowel Shift

Source: Clarke, Elms and Youssef 1995.

created a space into which /æ/ could move, which, in turn, created a space for /ɛ/ to retract and lower, which in turn led to the lowering of /ɪ/. This sequence of components of the shift received some support from the relative frequency of each component, with older components such as /æ/-retraction featuring higher rates of occurrence than newer components such as /ɪ/-lowering. Canadian English is also characterized by the fronting of /u/, but it's not clear whether this is part of the CVS or an independent development.

5.3 REGIONAL VARIATION

5.3.1 Studying Phonetic and Phonological Variation

As with lexical variation (see Chapter 4), variation in phonetic and phonological dialect features can be studied using surveys or questionnaires. In designing questions to elicit phonetic variants, it is important to remember that most people do not have any training in distinguishing phonetic detail or in phonetic transcription. If the questionnaire is not administered in person, so that responses can be transcribed by a trained phonetician, questions must be framed in such a way that the relevant phonetic distinctions can be inferred from responses. For example, to elicit variants in the pronunciation of the vowel in the word *soot* ([u] or [ʊ]), J.K. Chambers asked his respondents the question in (5.2).

(5.2)   Does SOOT (as in "chimney soot") rhyme with FOOT or BOOT?

If the questionnaire is administered in person, responses can not only be transcribed phonetically but audio-recorded for later analysis. In this case, rather than asking questions to elicit lexical items or rhyming judgments, it is more efficient to present the informant with a printed list of words to read, and then audio-record them as they read the list. Using a **word list** ensures that you obtain a sufficient amount of data from each informant, and that the phonetic environment is controlled for effects of surrounding sounds on the phonetic realization of the feature of interest. Word lists have a couple of disadvantages. If the informants have limited or no literacy, asking them to read a list of words may be embarrassing or challenging. Also, since reading a list of words is a highly unusual type of activity, the pronunciations elicited may not resemble the informant's behaviour in conversational interaction.

In order to overcome the unnaturalness involved in eliciting language data for phonetic and phonological analysis, other approaches have been used to approximate conversational interaction. As William Labov (1984) has noted, collecting sociolinguistic data involves two potentially conflicting goals: on the one hand, we want to collect data from a large, representative sample of the population we are studying; on the other hand, we want to collect data that is as close as possible to the way people speak when they are not being studied. Since most people command a range of speaking styles (from informal to formal), putting them in a situation where they know you are studying their speech is likely to elicit a more formal style. As a result, studies following on Labov's pioneering work in the 1960s have made use of the **sociolinguistic interview**, in which the researcher manipulates elements of the speech event to focus attention on content (i.e. what's being talked about) rather than on form (i.e. how it is being said). In conducting the sociolinguistic interview, the interviewer focuses on topics of interest to the informant—childhood games, neighbourhood life, memorable events, and so on. Most effective for the purposes of eliciting natural language data are **narratives** of personal experience, in which the informants become so caught up in retelling the story that they essentially relive the event (the most effective narratives, according to Labov, are those involving the danger of death). A sociolinguistic interview, which normally lasts between one and two hours, can provide dozens of realizations of the phonetic or phonological feature of interest. If the interviewer is successful in creating an informal context, the informant may approach the style of speaking that they normally use in conversational interaction with friends and family. While the sociolinguistic interview offers the advantage of heightened naturalism in the analysis of phonetic and phonological variation, it does have its limitations. The feature of interest may arise sporadically (or never) in the interview, and when it does occur, there is no controlling the phonetic contexts in which it occurs. These considerations mean that it may be difficult to compare data across speakers or communities.

5.3.2 Regional Variation in Canadian English

As noted at the beginning of this chapter, the Canadian English accent is often characterized as remarkably homogeneous, not exhibiting the distinctive regional variation found in the United Kingdom or even in the United States (Chambers 1998b). However, this characterization is really only true for GCE, and undoubtedly stems from the fact that the English-speaking areas of central and western Canada were settled primarily from or through Upper Canada (Ontario), with the variety of English spoken there serving as the model for subsequent arrivals (under the founder principle). However, as we saw in Chapter 3, the English-speaking regions of eastern Canada have undergone rather different patterns of settlement and immigration, suggesting that there should be regional variety in Canadian English outside of GCE.

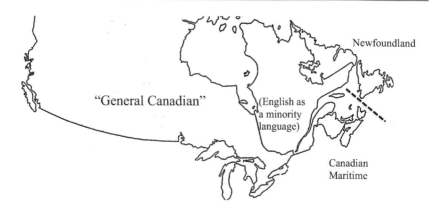

FIGURE 5.6 Traditional regional dialect areas of Canadian English

Source: Adapted from Trudgill 2000.

In addition, the characterization of GCE as homogeneous has until recently not been tested through large-scale sociophonetic analysis, which might reveal more complex patterns of social and linguistic conditioning not evident in more traditional methods of analysis.

A traditional view of the divisions of dialects within Canadian English within the context of North American English is shown in Figure 5.6 (adapted from Trudgill 2000): "General Canadian" is taken as stretching from the Ontario/Quebec border to the west coast, with Newfoundland (but not Labrador) and the Maritimes as two different dialect regions, and the province of Quebec excluded as a minority English-speaking region. Although this characterization of regional variation in Canadian English is becoming less tenable with ongoing work, I will take this as a starting point, examining each of these regions in turn, moving from east to west.

The regional variety of Canadian English that differs most markedly from GCE is undoubtedly Newfoundland and Labrador English (NLE; which includes not only the island of Newfoundland but the mainland part of the province), largely as a result of the province's unique patterns of settlement (almost entirely from southeastern Ireland and southwestern England) and its geographic isolation from the rest of the country (see Clarke 2010b; see Chapter 3). While the phonemic consonant inventory of NLE is not substantially different from that of GCE, the phonetic realization of consonants can vary quite a bit. In NLE, *th*-stopping is common, not only with the voiced phoneme /ð/ in function words, such as *the* and *there*, which occurs in some styles in other varieties of English, but also with the voiceless phoneme /θ/ more generally, so that the word *three* sounds like *tree*. In the Irish-settled parts of Newfoundland, the phoneme /l/ is realized as a clear [l] rather than the dark [ɫ] more common in

North American English, and is sometimes vocalized to [w]. In the English-settled parts of Newfoundland, deletion of initial /h/ is common (e.g. 'appy), which can also lead to h-insertion in words in which there is no etymological /h/ (e.g. h-early). Probably the most noticeable difference in consonants between NLE and GCE is the frequent realization of word-final /t/ with an affricated (or "slit") variant.

The vowel system of NLE is complicated by the coexistence of several systems, ranging from a province-wide "standard" accent to accents associated with regions of the province settled from Ireland and England. The primary phonetic realizations of standard NLE for the different lexical classes are shown in Table 5.3 (adapted from the characterizations provided by Wells [1982] and Clarke [2010a]), in which additional phonetic variants are indicated through the use of commas or parentheses. In general, the NLE vowel system is distinguished from that of GCE in the realizations of the low and low-back

TABLE 5.3

Phonetic Realizations of Lexical Classes of Standard Newfoundland English

KIT	ɪ	GOAT	ʌʊ
			ɔʊ
DRESS	ɛ	GOOSE	uː
TRAP/BATH	æ(ː)	PRICE	əɪ
			ɔɪ
LOT/CLOTH/	ɒ(ː)	CHOICE	ɔɪ
THOUGHT	a(ː)		əɪ
	ɑ(ː)		
STRUT	ʌ	MOUTH	aʊ
	ɔ̈		əʊ
FOOT	ʊ	NEAR	iːr
			ɛɹ
NURSE	ɚ	SQUARE	ɛɹ
	(ɔɹ)		
FLEECE	i	START	aɹ
			æɹ
FACE	ɛ	NORTH/FORCE	ɔɹ
	ɛɪ		(aɹ)
PALM	æ(ː)	CURE	ʊɹ
	ɑː		ɔɹ

Source: Adapted from Wells (1982) and Clarke (2010a)

vowels and the onsets of diphthongs and vowels before /r/. Both Canadian Raising (and fronting of the onset in /aw/) and the low-back vowel merger exist to varying degrees in different varieties of NLE, although the phonetic realization of the merged vowel is more fronted than in GCE, realized as [ɐ] or [a]. Vowels before /r/ in the START and NORTH classes also tend to be more fronted, as [a] or even [æ], and the onsets of diphthongs in the CHOICE and PRICE classes vary between more central [ə] and more backed [ɔ] realizations (see Clarke [2010b] for a more thorough discussion of the regional and stylistic variation in NLE vowels).

Until recently (Boberg 2010; Labov, Ash and Boberg 2006; see below) there has not been as much attention paid to the phonetics of Maritime English (ME), the varieties of English spoken in the Atlantic provinces other than Newfoundland—Nova Scotia, New Brunswick and Prince Edward Island. As in NLE, some varieties of ME (such as that spoken in the island of Cape Breton in Nova Scotia) show evidence of slit /t/. The palatalization of /s/ in consonant clusters with /tr/ and /kr/, so that *street* and *scream* begin with [ʃtɹ] and [ʃkɹ], respectively, has been noted in Nova Scotia and Prince Edward Island. The vowel systems of ME show a number of differences from both GCE and NLE (Kiefte and Kay-Raining Bird 2010). While there is evidence of the low-back vowel merger, its phonetic realization differs slightly from GCE, being rounder and more back, [ɒ] or [ɔ]. There is also little evidence for Canadian Raising in Maritime English: the onset of the diphthongs /ay/ and /aw/ tend to be realized in a more back and rounded form, as [ɒj] or [ɔw] (to my GCE ears, *about* in Nova Scotian English sounds like *a boat*). The low vowels in the START and TRAP classes tend to be fronted and somewhat raised and the FACE vowel is monophthongized.

Quebec English (QE) has until recently (see Boberg 2010 and below) also received little attention from phonetic analysis, presumably because the English-speaking population in this province constitutes a minority, as indicated in Figure 5.6, although this status belies the substantial *number* of English speakers in Quebec. Most work on QE focuses on Montreal, home to the largest English-speaking community in the province. The historical pattern of English-speaking settlement in Montreal is different from that in Ontario, in that the founding population does not trace back to Loyalist migration but to immigration directly from the United Kingdom in the 19th century. Montreal is also home to substantial and long-standing Jewish and Italian communities that shifted to English (see Chapter 7). Although not as substantial as in Montreal, there are other English-speaking communities in the province that can be traced back to the 1790s, notably the Eastern Townships (centred on the city of Sherbrooke) and in Quebec City.

As noted above, the majority of English-speaking Canada (in terms of both geography and population) is said to speak GCE, although this

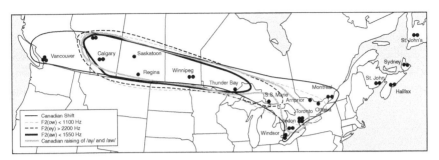

FIGURE 5.7 Regional distribution of the defining features of Canadian English phonology
Source: Map 15.7, Labov, Ash and Boberg 2006: 224.

generalization is normally restricted to "urban, middle-class anglophone Canadians" (Chambers 1998b:252). We might ask about the exact extent of the geographical range of GCE. We do not want to include the Atlantic provinces, but should QE be excluded, as in Figure 5.6? In the *Atlas of North American English* (Labov, Ash and Boberg 2006), which included a small number of informants from the largest Canadian cities, GCE is characterized on the basis of several defining features: the CVS (lowering and/or retraction of the front lax vowels), /ow/-fronting, /aw/-fronting and Canadian Raising (CR). As Figure 5.7 shows, the CVS extends across most of Canada (even part of the Atlantic provinces) but shows some variation. Using the CVS, we can define an area called "Inland Canada", whose outer limits extend from Vancouver to Montreal. Within Inland Canada is a smaller region, defined by the more traditional feature of Canadian Raising that includes the area from Alberta to northern Ontario. This characterization provides us with an overall picture of the extent of GCE's geographical distribution, but the study does not include sufficient number of speakers from each locale within Canada to explore the possibility of regional variation not only between GCE and the other Canadian dialect regions, but also within GCE.

In order to provide a more nuanced analysis of regional variation within Canadian English, a larger study was carried out by Charles Boberg (2008, 2010) through a word list administered to 86 students at McGill University in Montreal who originated from different parts of Canada. The normalized means of their vowels, shown in Figure 5.8, reveal the presence of the features characteristic of Canadian English. The CVS can be seen in the lowered and retracted positions of /i/, /e/ and /æ/ relative to the tense vowels /iy/ and /ey/. Both tense back vowels /uw/ and /ow/ exhibit fronting (shown in relation to their allophones before /l/), and the onset of /aw/ tends to be fronted with respect to the onset of /ay/. Canadian Raising can be seen in the higher position of the onsets of /awT/ and /ayT/ (where the T indicates a following voiceless consonant) relative to /aw/ and /ay/.

The vowel means presented in Figure 5.8 represent the combined measurements for all 86 informants, regardless of the region of Canada they come from. Table 5.4 displays the vowel measurements that were found to have a

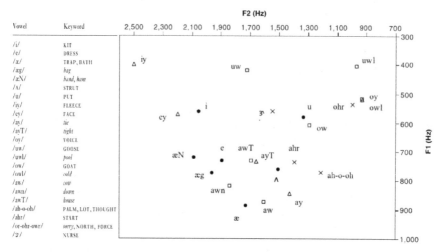

FIGURE 5.8 Mean acoustic vowel measurements in Canadian English

Source: Boberg 2010: 144–45.

TABLE 5.4

Means Acoustic Measurements (Hz) for Vowel Features of Canadian English with Significant Regional Effects (bold and italic indicate different directions of effect)

	BC	Prairies	Ontario			QC	Maritimes	NL
			South	Toronto	East			
F1(awT)	**736**	**732**	**716**	**685**	**691**	*776*	**718**	*826*
F2(awT)	*1636*	*1612*	**1770**	**1784**	**1757**	**1705**	**1702**	**1750**
F2(uw)	**1804**	*1657*	**1895**	**1827**	*1769*	*1751*	*1652*	*1546*
F2(ow)	**1337**	*1227*	*1258*	**1352**	**1350**	*1288*	*1269*	*1226*
F2(ahr)	*1298*	*1313*	**1396**	**1428**	**1443**	*1339*	**1509**	**1524**
F1(æN)	*741*	*742*	**693**	**670**	**653**	*761*	**696**	*806*
F2(æg)	**2008**	**2103**	*1927*	*1912*	*1972*	*1862*	*1978*	*1896*

Source: Adapted from Table 5.4, Boberg 2010: 204

TABLE 5.5

Significance and Distribution of Features in Regional Varieties of Canadian English

Feature	Significant?	GCE			QE	ME	NLE
		BC	PR	ON			
Canadian Raising (F1 awT)	yes	+	+	+	−	+	−
/u/-fronting	(no)	+	−	+	−	−	−
/o/-fronting	yes	+	−	+	−	−	−
Canadian Raising (F2 awT)	yes	−	−	+	−	−	−
Unretracted /ahr/	yes	−	−	+	−	+	+
/æN/-raising	yes	−	−	+	−	+	−
/æg/-raising	yes	+	+	−	−	−	−
Canadian Vowel Shift	no						
/aw/-fronting	no						

Source: Adapted from Table 5.5, Boberg 2010: 203, 209

statistically significant effect for region, summarized graphically in Table 5.5. Note that these regional differences confirm some of the generalizations about larger regions within Canadian English made in the preceding section. The CVS is not significantly different according to region, suggesting that this feature occurs across the entire country. Fronting of /u/ is marginally nonsignificant, which indicates that there may be some slight regional effects. NLE shows itself to be distinct from other regions in its lack of participation in Canadian Raising (indicated by a high F1 value for /awT/, which signals a much lower vowel) and /uw/- and /ow/-fronting (indicated by lower F2 values for /uw/). ME patterns with GCE in participating in Canadian Raising, but it patterns with NLE in not retracting /a/ before /r/. QE does not partici- pate in any of the other phonetic process in other regions. While all varieties of GCE feature Canadian Raising (at least, raising of /aw/ rather than /ay/), Tables 5.4 and 5.5 also reveal some subtle differences between regions. The English spoke in BC and Ontario both feature /u/-fronting, which does not occur in the Prairies. However, the Prairies and BC pattern together against Ontario with respect to raising of /æ/ before velar consonants and the (lack of) fronting of raised /awT/.

SUMMARY

This chapter considered the sound system of Canadian English, in terms of its phonological systems and their phonetic realizations. Canadian English is distinguished from other varieties of English on the basis of its vowel phonemes, which results from various mergers and shifts. Its main features are the low-back vowel merger, Canadian Raising and the Canadian Vowel shift. Regionally, Canadian English can be divided into several dialect areas: General Canadian English, Quebec English, Maritime English and Newfoundland English. Phonetic analysis reveals subtle distinctions between and even within these regions.

6

Grammatical Variation

6.0 INTRODUCTION

The previous chapter discussed the phonetic and phonological features of Canadian English and regional variation in the phonetic realization of consonant and vowel features. We also considered some of the methodological and analytical issues involved in studying phonetic variation, as well as principles of vowel shifts and mergers and how these operate in different varieties of Canadian English.

In this chapter, we turn to the features of Canadian English above and beyond the lexicon and sound systems. Here I am using the term *grammatical* to cover a wide range of areas of the linguistic system: morphological, syntactic and discourse-pragmatic. Despite the fact that each of these subsystems constitutes whole fields of study within linguistics, one reason for including them within one chapter is that they often interact with each other in various ways, so that it may be difficult to discern where one field leaves off and another starts. Also, in some cases a feature in one area (say, morphology) may be conditioned by considerations in another area (such as discourse-pragmatics). Another reason is that the methods of studying variation in morphology, syntax and discourse-pragmatics involve similar considerations of data collection and analysis.

Unlike lexical and phonetic features, which speakers of English are generally aware of to some degree and serve to mark people as coming from different regional backgrounds, grammatical features are less salient in identifying regional or social differences. In fact, it may be argued that most dialects of English do not differ greatly in their grammatical systems. For Canadian English, grammatical features are probably even more homogeneous across the country than are phonological or phonetic features. However, as we saw with phonetic variation, in some cases there may be fine-grained differences between varieties that are not readily apparent but can only be discovered through detailed analysis. So, we need to be concerned not only with the presence or absence of a particular grammatical feature, but also with how frequently it is used and how it is conditioned by the social and linguistic context.

In this chapter, I begin by outlining some of the methodological and analytical issues involved in studying grammatical variation. As in the previous chapter, I will first discuss the features of General Canadian English (GCE), the variety spoken by most (urban, middle-class anglophone) English speakers in Canada from eastern Ontario to Vancouver Island, before turning to a discussion of regional features. I will then illustrate with studies that have been conducted on grammatical variables in Canadian English.

6.1 GRAMMATICAL FEATURES OF GENERAL CANADIAN ENGLISH

Unlike lexical and phonetic and phonological features, grammatical variation does not generally serve to distinguish varieties of English. There are a few features of the grammar and discourse of Canadian English that differentiate it from some other varieties of English, but most of these cannot be said to be unique to Canadian English.

Varieties of English differ with respect to how they treat main-verb *have*. As we saw in Chapter 2, auxiliary and modal verbs in English can be fronted in questions and negative statements (6.1). Main verbs cannot be fronted, and rely on the use of a dummy auxiliary verb *do* to carry the tense and agreement marking (6.2).

(6.1)   a. *Hecubus is eating.* *Hecubus isn't eating.*   *Is Hecubus eating?*
        b. *Hecubus has eaten.* *Hecubus hasn't eaten.* *Has Hecubus eaten?*
        c. *Hecubus can eat.*   *Hecubus can't eat.*   *Can Hecubus eat?*
(6.2)   *Hecubus eats.*   **Hecubus eats not.*   **Eats Hecubus?*
                   Hecubus does not eat. *Does Hecubus eat?*

For main-verb *have*, the sentences in (6.3) are all possible, though the sentences in (6.3a) are more common in British English, while those in (6.3b) are preferred in North American English.

(6.3)   a. *You have a cat.* *You haven't a cat.*   *Have you a cat?*
        b. *You have a cat.* *You don't have a cat.* *Do you have a cat?*

Although this variable feature of English only affects a single lexical item, and might be better considered a lexical variable, as it affects only a single lexical item, it holds consequences for the verb phrase. Possession may also be indicated with a third variant, the periphrastic construction *have got*, in which the *have* may be omitted (6.4).

(6.4)   *You have a cat.   You've got a cat.   Have you got a cat?*
                         I got a cat.   You got a cat?

Variation in main-verb *have* is reflected in the expression of deontic modality (see Chapter 2), in which an action is suggested or required (6.5). Here, not only the same range of variants of *have* is possible, but also the older modal *must* (6.5d).

(6.5)   a. *You have to see this!*
        b. *You have got to see this! You've got to see this!*
        c. *You got to (gotta) see this!*
        d. *You must see this!*

Variation in the form of *have* with a modal also exists in counterfactual constructions (expressing the possibility of something contrary to fact), where a preterit *had* or a construction with modal *would* are both possible (6.6).

(6.6)   a. *If I had known you were coming, I'd have baked a cake.*
        b. *If I would have known you were coming, I'd have baked a cake.*

Outside of *have*, variation in verbal morphology is not particularly common in Canadian English. In some contexts the preterit is used where the past participle would be expected, as in (6.7).

(6.7)   *If I had knew you were coming, . . .*

More common is variation between the "singular" and "plural" morphology of *be* in constructions with *there* when the postverbal subject is plural, as in (6.8).

(6.8)   a. *There are bears back there.*
        b. *There is bears back there.*
        c. *There's bears back there.*

This is the only area in which Canadian English shows any variability in the verbal morphology of subject-verb agreement (see below for a more detailed discussion). With pronouns there is variation in conjoined NPs between a standard construction imposed through formal education and constructions in which the object form is used in subject position (6.9), which may be

responsible for the occurrence of "hypercorrect" forms in the object position
(6.10).

(6.9)   a. *Me and Sali went to the movies.*
        b. *Sali and I went to the movies.*
(6.10) a. *There was a discussion between me and Sali.*
        b. *There was a discussion between Sali and I.*

Finally, predicate adjectives are variably intensified with a variety of forms:
very, really, so and so forth (6.11). This is an area in which there do seem to
be differences between varieties of English, as Canadian English does not use
intensifiers such as *dead* or *wicked*, found in other varieties of English.

(6.11) *That movie was <u>very</u> ~ <u>really</u> ~ so good.*

There is more variability in Canadian English at the level of discourse-
pragmatics, though again it is not clear the extent to which any of these features can be said to be unique to Canadian English. Particularly notable here is
the incursion into the system of quotation through the use of the construction
be like, as in (6.12).

(6.12) *So I said/say ~ went/go ~ 'm/was like, "Where are you going?"*

This feature will be considered in more detail below.

Perhaps the most remarked on discourse feature of Canadian English is the
purportedly high use of the utterance-final discourse marker *eh*, which has
received notice in popular culture. There are several ongoing questions about
eh, such as whether it is exclusively Canadian, how frequently Canadians actually use it, and whether its use is in decline. Walter Avis (1972), who claimed
that the frequency of *eh* in Canadian English was so high among some individuals that it posed a threat to communication (Avis 1972: 103), identified
eight uses of *eh*:

1. A simple request for repetition (with rising intonation) to indicate that
    something was not heard, to indicate that something was not fully under-
    stood (suggesting surprise or disbelief) or to indicate preoccupation: *Eh?*
2. The equivalent of a tag question (with rising intonation), occurring at the
    end of a statement: *It's a hot day, eh? (It's a hot day, isn't it?)*
3. Soliciting agreement in a negative response (similar to 2): *It's not too hot
    out, eh? (It's not too hot out, is it?)*
4. Reinforcing an exclamation (with rising intonation): *What a day, eh!*

5. Reinforcing an imperative: *Pass me the salt, eh?*
6. Reinforcing an interrogative (with rising intonation): *Who's that guy, eh?*
7. Reinforcing an interrogative in nonfinal position (with level intonation).
8. "Narrative eh":

> *So I went to the game yesterday, eh?*
> *But there were no tickets available, eh?*
> *So I saw a scalper outside, eh?*
> *And he wanted 100 bucks!*

Avis suggested that it is perhaps only this last use of *eh* that is uniquely Canadian (although, as we will see below, *eh* may be giving way to other discourse markers such as *right* [Tagliamonte 2006a]).

Just as Canadian English is not generally differentiated from other varieties of English through its grammatical features, as far as we know, there is not a great deal of regional variation in grammatical features within Canadian English. One exception to this general statement is Newfoundland and Labrador English (NLE), some varieties of which are notable in departing quite radically from the grammar of mainstream North American English. One such feature is *pronoun exchange*, in which "subject"-form pronouns are used in object position (6.13) and "object"-form pronouns are used in subject position (6.14) (all of the examples in this paragraph are taken from Clarke [2010b]).

(6.13) a. *There was a lot of they around.*
      b. *I'll always remember he.*
(6.14) a. *"Where's us goin'?" he said.*
      b. *Is 'em (them) goin' to get any?*

NLE also exhibits variation in the verb phrase, with habitual constructions such as *do be* (6.15), where the *do* is unstressed and pronounced [də], common in the English-settled parts of the island and *bes* (6.16) common in the Irish-settled communities.

(6.15) *I do be so hungry I don't know where I'm at.*
(6.16) *I bes home all the time.*

Very noticeable in NLE verb constructions is the "recent past" *after*-perfect, which has clear antecedents in Irish English (6.17).

(6.17) *I'm just after seeing him.* (= *I've just seen him.*)

NLE features greater variability in subject-verb agreement, not only in plural existential constructions. Verbal –s may occur with other grammatical persons and numbers (6.18).

(6.18) a. *I always calls him Joseph, see.*
       b. *You looks like Sarah.*

Also unlike GCE, NLE features distinctive intensifiers, notably *fair* and *some*. Perhaps the most salient discourse feature of Newfoundland and Labrador English is the use of ingressive *yeah*, pronounced by drawing air into the lungs rather than by expelling air. See Chapters 3 and 4 of Sandra Clarke's (2010b) book *Newfoundland and Labrador English*.

Another exception to the generalization that Canadian English is not distinguished by regional variation in grammatical structure is the variety spoken by Nova Scotians of African American descent. As we saw in Chapter 3, the Loyalist exodus from post-revolutionary New York in 1783 included 3,000 Black Loyalists. Although about half of them volunteered to be resettled in Africa, the remaining population established communities that still exist. As a result of the geographic and social isolation these communities underwent until relatively recently, they have preserved many of the distinctive grammatical features of African American English that differentiate them from the surrounding populations (Poplack and Tagliamonte 1991/1993, 2001). Among these features are variable absence of the verb *be*, as in (6.19a), variable marking of subject-verb agreement with –s (6.19b) and variable marking of past tense on verbs (6.19c) (examples from Walker 2000 and Poplack and Tagliamonte 1991/1993).

(6.19) a. *She always eating banana sandwich.*
       b. *If I go to a lake in- uh- in a car and a lake is handy, I gets all nerved up.*
       c. *When I look in like that, and I look in that door, and I look back in the corner, I seen them great big eye.*

See Shana Poplack and Sali Tagliamonte's (2001) book *African American English in the Diaspora* for more detailed discussion of African Nova Scotian English.

6.2 STUDYING GRAMMATICAL VARIATION

Unlike lexical and phonetic and phonological variation, grammatical variation is less amenable to study through the use of dialect questionnaires. One exception to this statement is morphological variation in the realization of particular lexical items, such as the past tense of *dive* as *dived* or *dove*. However, many of the most interesting grammatical and discourse features are difficult to study through elicitation. For example, respondents to the *Survey of Vancouver English* (Gregg et al. 2004) largely rejected the use of *eh* in their responses, which seems unlikely based on casual observation. Elaine Gold and Mireille Tremblay (2006) conducted a survey of undergraduate students at the University of Toronto and Laval University on the use of *eh* and *hein* in different contexts, but they relied on self-reported usage and attitudes toward the discourse markers rather than studying usage directly. For these reasons, studies of grammatical variation tend to rely on large corpora of publically available data or sociolinguistic interviews, although in some cases the grammatical or discourse feature may not occur frequently enough to make quantitative analysis possible.

The central problem in studying grammatical variation is determining whether different forms actually mean "the same thing". This consideration, which is less controversial in studies of lexical or phonetic variation, makes it difficult to test claims about frequency and the conditioning of the variation. Some studies attempt to "normalize" the occurrence of features by calculating rates per hour of speech or 10,000 words of text, but this approach relies on the assumption that the feature occurs at regular intervals. Another approach is to identify a particular grammatical context or function and calculate the rates of covariation among forms that occur in that domain. In part, because of such considerations, we cannot draw on as much information in delimiting regional variation (either between Canadian English and other varieties of English, or within Canada) as we can for lexical or phonetic variation.

For lexical variation, we defined a Canadianism as a lexical item that can either trace its origin to Canada or that is used at higher rates or with a unique meaning in Canada. If we extend the notion of Canadianism into the realm of grammar, we could distinguish between grammatical features that differ between Canadian English and other varieties. J.K. Chambers (2004) noted the occurrence of a number of features in nonstandard spoken varieties of English around the world that could not have arisen independently of each other, which he dubbed "vernacular universals". For example, in many spoken varieties of English, there are processes of morphological regularization, in which irregular forms become regularized, as in the use of the past participle in preterit contexts (*I seen him* for *I saw him*, *I been there* for *I was there*). This morphological regularization also occurs with subject-verb agreement, where default singulars can develop (such as *we was* or the variation between *there is* and *there are* discussed above). Other features include multiple negation (*I haven't seen nothing*) and copula absence (*She bad*). An interesting question that arises from the notion of vernacular universals is whether such features are equivalent in all varieties or whether the use of such features is conditioned in the same way by social and linguistic features. If so, a comparative analysis of the same feature in different communities should help to determine whether in fact there are any distinctions among varieties of English in the occurrence of vernacular universals (see Section 6.3.1 below).

Another source of differences between grammars arises through ongoing processes of **grammaticalization**. Linguists distinguish between *lexical*, or content, words, which refer to things or activities or states in the world outside of language, and *function* words, which are purely language-internal. As we saw in Chapter 4, new content words enter the language all the time—they can be invented or borrowed. In contrast, it is much less common for new function words to be invented or borrowed. *Grammaticalization* (a term originally attributed to Antoine Meillet in 1912) is a kind of language change in which a lexical form (a word or morpheme) takes on grammatical function. The most commonly cited example of this process is the development in English (also in French, Spanish and Portuguese, as well as other languages) of a verb of motion, *go*, into a marker of the future, *be going to*. More recent work has widened the definition beyond this canonical type of grammaticalization to include examples in which forms that are already grammatical move into other areas of the grammar.

Research on grammaticalization (Bybee et al. 1993; Hopper 1991) has discovered several principles that make predictions about the trajectory of change. The *principle of layering* states that multiple forms can undergo grammaticalization into the same function. This principle accounts for the covariance of forms expressing the future that grammaticalized at different times in the past. For example, the modal future *will*, which grammaticalized from an Old English verb *willan* ("to want to", covaries with the grammaticalized *be going to* future, which, as mentioned above, grammaticalized from a verb of motion.

Because grammaticalization does not happen suddenly but operates over long periods of time (the first example of the *going to* future in English dates to the 15th century), two (potentially contradictory) tendencies are involved. Under the *principle of persistence* (or *retention*), forms that undergo grammaticalization retain semantic nuances inherited from their lexical sources. For example, the *go*-future retains some traces of its origin as a verb of motion. In contrast, under the *principles of semantic bleaching* (or *desemanticization*) and the *principle of erosion* (or *phonetic reduction*), grammaticalizing forms gradually lose the semantic content and phonetic structure of their lexical source and undergo contraction and coalescence. Finally, under the *principle of syntactic generalization,* grammaticalizing forms become more open in the syntactic contexts in which they can occur and lose subcategorical information (changing grammatical category and from open to closed class). These last three principles predict that persistence or retention will weaken over time as the grammaticalizing form becomes phonetically reduced, semantically bleached and syntactically less restricted. Both *going to* and *will* have phonetically reduced forms (*gonna* and *'ll*) and appear to have lost much of their original semantic content (motion and volition, respectively). Thus, if we examine processes of grammaticalization, we expect forms undergoing this process to exhibit these features (see Section 6.3.2 below).

6.3 GRAMMATICAL VARIATION IN CANADIAN ENGLISH

6.3.1 Variable Agreement with Plural Existentials

As noted above, one of the few areas of the grammar in which Canadian English exhibits morphological variation is in existential constructions with plural reference, which vary between plural agreement and singular agreement. This feature has been offered by Chambers (2004) as an example of a vernacular universal. Studies of this feature agree that singular agreement is more likely in the present tense (especially with contracted *'s*), in negatives, with subjects that are separated from *be* and if the NP subject lacks the plural *–s*. Most attention has been paid to the type of determiner occurring in the postverbal subject NP (see examples in (6.20)). As Figure 6.1 shows, the effect of the determiner differs across varieties of English.

Canada	*no* > Number > Other
Falkland Islands	*no* > Number > Definite > Bare > Quantifier > Adjective
New Zealand	*a* > *no* > Definite > Number > Bare > Quantifier > Adjective
	Number > *no* > *a* > Definite > Bare > Quantifier > Adjective
United Kingdom	*no* > Partitive > Definite > Number > Quantifier > Bare

FIGURE 6.1 Effect of determiner type on singular agreement in plural existentials (more > less) in different varieties of English

Source: Adapted from Figure 1, Walker 2007: 153.

(8) a. No determiner: *There's bears back there.*
     b. Adjective: *There are young people.*
     c. Definite article: *'Cause there was the football players that lived there.*
     d. *a:*   *There's a lot of separatists.*
     e. *lots:*   *Oh well there's lots of things that you can't translate.*
     f. no: *And there were no schools here.*
     g. Number: *There's two kinds of pension.*

In a study of this feature in Quebec English, I noted that the form *there's*, which always has singular agreement, tends to occur very frequently, so that including it in the analysis might be skewing overall rates. As a result, I first analyzed singular agreement without *there's* (that is, *there is* vs. *there are*), before examining what conditions the occurrence of *there's*.

Table 6.1 shows a multivariate analysis of the linguistic factors conditioning the occurrence of singular agreement in Quebec English. Each of the decimal numbers is a factor weight (see p. 31 in Chapter 2) that indicates the relative contribution made to *there's* by each factor when all factors are considered together. Factor weights range between 0 and 1, with higher values indicating a favoring effect on *there's*. The greatest effect (indicated by its range) is that of past tense, though all factor groups except

TABLE 6.1

**Factors Contributing to the Occurrence of
Singular Agreement in Plural Existentials in
Quebec City English (excluding *there's*)**

Total N:	946
Input:	.526
Tense	
Past	.60
Present	.18
Range:	*42*
Plural –s	
Absent	.63
Present	.37
Range:	*26*
Extension Beyond NP	
Adverb	.64
None	.53
Phrase	.43
Range:	*21*
Intervening Material	
Present	.64
Absent	.48
Range:	*16*

Source: Walker 2007

determiner type and extension are selected as significant. Although not significant, if we examine the effects of different determiner types (as in Figure 6.2), we
see similarities between the relative ranking here and those of other studies.

Once we return *there's* to the analysis, determiner type is selected as significant (Table 6.2). However, the relative ranking in Table 6.2 is quite different
from that for singular agreement in Table 6.1, illustrated in Figure 6.3.

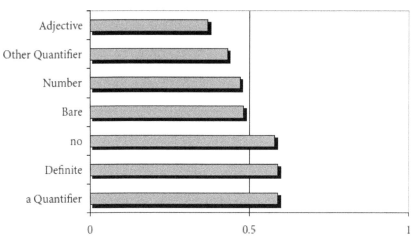

FIGURE 6.2 Effect of determiner type (not significant) on singular agreement with plural
existentials in Quebec City English

Source: Adapted from Figure 2, Walker 2007: 159.

TABLE 6.2

Factors Contributing to the Occurrence of *there's*
in Plural Existentials in Quebec City English

Total N:	1688
Input:	.438
Type of Determiner	
'a' Quantifier	.65
Adjective	.55
Bare	.49
Negative	.48
Definite	.46
Number	.39
Other Quantifier	.39
Range:	25
Intervening Material	
Present	.58
Absent	.49
Range:	9

Source: Walker 2007

Canada	*no* > Number > Other
	a > Definite > Negative > Bare > Number > Quantifier > Adjective
	a > Adjective > Bare > Negative > Definite > Number > Quantifier
Falkland Islands	*no* > Number > Definite > Bare > Quantifier > Adjective
New Zealand	*a* > *no* > Definite > Number > Bare > Quantifier > Adjective
	Number > *no* > *a* > Definite > Bare > Quantifier > Adjective
United Kingdom	*no* > Partitive > Definite > Number > Quantifier > Bare

FIGURE 6.3 Effect of determiner type on singular agreement (more > less) in different varieties of English, revised

Source: Figure 3, Walker 2007: 161.

Thus, a cross-variety comparison of the linguistic factors conditioning the occurrence of singular agreement in plural existentials reveals more similarities than differences, offering little evidence for regionalisms and support for the idea of singular agreement as a vernacular universal.

6.3.2 *Quotative* be Like

As noted above, a recent newcomer to the discourse-pragmatic system of Canadian English is the entry of *be like* into the system of quotation, which has largely ousted the more traditional variants. The coexistence of multiple variants drawn from different lexical sources illustrates clearly the principle of layering in grammaticalization. We might then ask whether the other principles of grammaticalization are operative, by examining the conditioning of *be like* by language-internal factors. Previous studies have found that *be like* is favoured for first person subjects and for introducing internal thought, perhaps a persistence of its original function of imitating nonlexicalized sounds.

In the early 2000s, Sali Tagliamonte and Alexandra D'Arcy (2004) collected and analyzed quotative strategies used by young English speakers in Toronto between the ages of 10 and 19 years. The overall distribution of quotatives is shown in Table 6.3. Note that the newest form *be like* occupies the majority of tokens (58%), while the next most frequent options, zero and *say*, occur at only 18% and 11%, respectively. This distribution suggests a drastic reorganization of the quotative system in Canadian English, in which verbs of saying have been replaced by the *be like* construction.

If *be like* is a rapid newcomer to the system of quotation, we should expect to see differences among speakers according to their time of acquisition. Table 6.4 shows

TABLE 6.3

Overall Distribution of Quotative Verbs in
Young Toronto English

Quotative Verb	%	N
be like	58	1198
Zero	18	362
say	11	227
go	7	136
think	2	34
Other	5	101
Total		2058

Source: Tagliamonte and D'Arcy 2004

TABLE 6.4

Contribution of Social and Language-Internal Factors to the Occurrence
of Quotative *be like* in Young Toronto English, by Age Group

	10–14 years	15–16 years	17–19 years
Input:	.53	.67	.71
Total N:	535	449	967
Sex			
Female	.52	.56	.57
Male	.45	.40	.37
Range	7	16	20
Grammatical person			
First	.64	.58	.58
Third	.48	.45	.43
Range	17	13	15
Content of the quote			
Internal dialogue	.57	.63	.42
Direct speech	.47	.47	.53
Range	10	16	11

Source: Adapted from Tagliamonte and D'Arcy 2004

three multivariate analyses of the contribution of one social factor (sex) and the
two linguistic factors (grammatical person and content of the quote) to the choice
of *be like* (with factor weights ranging from 0 to 1) for three age groups among
the speakers. All three age groups display the same conditioning for grammatical
person and sex, with first-person subjects and females favouring *be like*. However,
the effect of the content of the quote is not constant: although internal thought

favours *be like* in the younger groups, it reverses in the 17–19 age group, where direct speech favours *be like*. Note that the relative strength of the factors within each analysis (indicated by the range) also changes across age groups. Although grammatical person remains constant across all age groups, the sex effect, which is weakest, with the youngest age group becomes the strongest effect in the oldest group. The effect of the content of the quote shifts dramatically, from a moderate to strong effect to the weakest constraint in the oldest group.

These results seem to reflect the pathway of grammaticalization followed by *be like* as it works its way into the quotative system, both in terms of its increasing frequency (revealed by the increasing input value at the top of each column) and in the way that the weighting of constraints changes. The origins of *be like* in its pragmatic function dominates among the youngest speakers, who presumably are just starting to acquire the feature. This effect first strengthens in the middle group before falling to the weakest constraint in the oldest group, suggesting that the association of *be like* with internal dialogue weakens as its development and use proceeds.

SUMMARY

This chapter discussed the grammatical features of Canadian English, including morphological, syntactic and discourse-pragmatic features. Although grammatical features are less salient and may not serve to distinguish varieties of English in the same way that phonetic and lexical features do, detailed quantitative analysis may reveal regional differences that are not readily apparent. We considered a number of features that differentiate between North American English and other varieties, as well as several other features that may distinguish Canadian English. We also looked at two varieties of English spoken in Canada that show marked grammatical differences from other varieties: Newfoundland and Labrador English and African Nova Scotian English.

We also discussed some of the methodological differences between studying phonetic and lexical variation and studying grammatical variation, which make survey methods less useful. Grammatical variation challenges our understanding of the linguistic variable. One question in grammatical variation is whether grammatical features can be considered regionalisms or whether they are universal to all English vernaculars. Another source of differences between grammars of English is the process of grammaticalization. I illustrated these questions through two empirical studies of variation in Canadian English, one concerning variable agreement in existentials, the other an examination of the grammaticalization of quotative *be like*.

7

The Present and the Future of Canadian English

7.0 INTRODUCTION

The last few chapters presented an overview of the structural features of Canadian English. We examined lexical, phonetic and phonological, grammatical and discourse-pragmatic features and the similarities and differences between Canadian English and other varieties of English, as well as considered regional variation within the English-speaking communities of Canada. We also paid some attention to the different methods of data collection and analysis and their suitability for studying regional variation.

This chapter examines other ways in which the features of Canadian English are subject to variation, with a focus on social factors other than region. The first section looks at the relationship between linguistic variation and change, and discusses some of the analytical and methodological issues involved in studying language change: specifically, the use of social factors such as age and sex to understand how languages change, and when and how to differentiate between situations of stable variation and changes in progress. In the second section, we turn to another social factor, that of ethnicity. Given the rapid changes that have taken place in the ethnolinguistic composition of the English-speaking population of Canada over the last 50 years (see Chapter 3), especially in its largest cities, an interesting question is whether these changes hold linguistic consequences for the structural features we have discussed in the last few chapters. Incorporating ethnicity as a social factor in our accounts of language variation and change provide a deeper understanding of the nature of language change, and the future of Canadian English.

7.1 LANGUAGE VARIATION AND CHANGE

7.1.1 Studying Language Variation and Change

Language is always changing. You may have noticed that you speak differently from your parents and grandparents, and if you go further back in time, to read the writings of Charles Dickens (19th century) or William Shakespeare (late 16th to early 17th centuries), you will notice changes in spelling, pronunciation (evident in poetry), vocabulary and even in grammatical structure. Go even further back, to the writings of Geoffrey Chaucer (14th century) or the texts in Old English (or Anglo-Saxon) from the 6th to 10th centuries, and it seems that you are reading a different language, incomprehensible without the aid of dictionaries and grammars. Many people take a prescriptivist view toward language change, viewing the language in the past as inherently better and current language to be corrupt. Linguists take a descriptive view, not claiming that language becomes better or worse over time. What we want to know is *why* and *how* languages change.

Current interest in language change stems from the **philology** of the 18th and 19th centuries, which was concerned with establishing the historical relationships between living and dead languages, usually through the analysis of texts from languages that were no longer spoken, such as Latin, Ancient Greek, Old English, Old Norse and so on. Where such texts did not exist, such as the aboriginal languages of North America, philologists and linguists applied the same methods of historical reconstruction to figure out the history and relationships of different languages. By the middle of the 20th century, linguists could be fairly confident in their use of the historical comparative method to infer language change. However, it was commonly accepted that language change could only be observed after the fact. Looking at a language at one point in time, there was no way to know what changes were going on, and where they would go in the future.

It was not until the 1960s, when linguists such as William Labov and Charles-James Bailey began to study linguistic variation systematically, that the link between variation and change was recognized. Regardless of the theory of language change, all must acknowledge that change proceeds gradually; that is, speakers do not all go to bed one night speaking one way and wake up the next morning speaking differently. In the change from feature x to feature y, there is always a period in which x and y coexist. Over time, x is used less and less frequently and y is used more frequently, until only y remains. However, while all change requires variation, not all variation necessarily indicates change— the possibility of stable variation means that features may covary without one ousting the other. For example, the variation between –*ing* and –*in'* in words like *singing* has been traced as far back as Old English, and shows no sign of changing (Labov 1989).

With the advent of the variationist approach, and its recognition of the inherent variability of language, came the possibility of incorporating variation, and therefore ongoing change, into the study of language. The important question for variationists is how to recognize whether a particular situation of variation represents an ongoing change or stable variation. In a seminal paper published in 1968, Uriel Weinreich, William Labov and Marvin Herzog laid out five "problems" (really, questions) that any empirical account of language change must resolve:

1. *The Constraints Problem*: Given the state of a language at a particular time, what changes are possible, and what linguistic conditions drive the change?
2. *The Transition (or Incrementation) Problem*: How does each generation acquire the change from the preceding generation, and how do they drive the change forward?
3. *The Embedding Problem*: Social and linguistic forces may also drive language change. What are the social and linguistic contexts in which the change takes place, and what forces act to drive the change?
4. *The Evaluation Problem*: What do speakers think about the change (if they are aware of it), and what role does speaker attitude play in promoting or inhibiting change?
5. *The Actuation Problem*: At some point in time, something new is introduced to the language, and the change begins. How does this introduction happen? Why does the change begin when it does?

This last problem is perhaps the most difficult to address—we would be very lucky to observe the first use of a new form or feature in the language. At best we can try to reconstruct the early stages of a change by tracing it back to its beginnings. The other problems involve an understanding not only of the structural aspects of the language, but also its social context. The methodology of sociolinguistics has been developed specifically to address these problems.

Ideally, studying language change would involve making observations of a language as used in the speech community over different points in time—study the community at one point, wait 10, 20 or 30 years and study the community again. This type of **real-time** study is relatively rare, for practical reasons. The type of reliable audio-recording technology required was only developed within the last 100 years. The audio-recorded and written linguistic data that survives from the past is not always of the highest quality. Moreover, because literacy was until recently limited to a very small segment of society, the data that has survived is not representative of the full sociolinguistic range that would have existed in the past.

Such restrictions have led studies of sociolinguistic variation to rely on the assumption of **apparent time**: the distribution across speakers of different ages at one point in time can be taken to reflect states of the language at different points in time (what Labov has called "using the present to explain the past"). Apparent time assumes that speakers acquire their linguistic system before adolescence and that it remains unchanged across their lifespan. For example, a woman who turned 75 in 2014 and was born in 1939 in Toronto would therefore have acquired her linguistic system of English in the 1940s, and her speech now can be taken to represent Canadian English as it was spoken at that time.

The apparent-time construct has been questioned, because there remains the possibility that speakers can change across the course of their lifespan. Of course we can always learn new words, so the lexicon is particularly susceptible to change across the lifespan, but it is an ongoing question as to whether the phonological and grammatical systems, once acquired, can change. The possibility of **age-grading**, in which individual speakers change the way they speak according to their stage of life (often under normative pressure in adulthood) means that we cannot automatically infer that differences between age groups at any one point in time represent an ongoing change. The only way to definitively show that a change is in progress is through a real-time analysis.

There are a few real-time studies that have returned at a later point in time to conduct a follow-up study of the same community (a **trend** study), in some cases even rerecording the same speakers (a **panel** study). For example, the French-speaking community in Montreal studied by Henrietta Cedergren and Gillian Sankoff in 1971 (Sankoff and Cedergren 1972) was restudied by Pierrette Thibault and Diane Vincent in 1984 and again in 1991 (Thibault and Daveluy 1989; Vincent, Laforest and Martel 1995), including some of the speakers from the original study. Such studies have identified different scenarios of language change, depicted in Table 7.1. First, if neither the community nor the individual exhibits change, the variation must be stable. Age-grading occurs if individual speakers change across their lifespans but the community remains the same; that is, since every individual goes through

TABLE 7.1

Different Situations of Language Change, Depending on Whether the Community and the Individual Speaker's Linguistic System Remain Stable or Undergo Change

		INDIVIDUAL	
		Stable	Change
COMMUNITY	Stable	Stable variation	Age-grading
	Change	Generational change	Communal change

the same pattern in each generation, returning to the community at any point in time will show the same distribution according to age. If the community exhibits change but individuals remain stable throughout their lifespan, we are dealing with generational change, and the assumption of apparent time holds. Finally, speakers may change across their lifespan at the same time that the community is changing. Real-time studies have found that this final pattern, **communal change**, involves speakers increasing the frequency of an incoming form across their lifespan, even after childhood, in concert with an increase in frequency across the community; that is, when individuals do change, they do it in the same direction as the community. In fact, Sankoff and Blondeau (2007) have suggested that the apparent-time construct may even underestimate the extent to which individual speakers change in the same direction as the community.

Studies of language change have also found social factors to be indicative of change in progress. Some changes begin in higher social classes before being adopted by lower social classes (**change from above**), while other changes originate in lower social classes and percolate upwards (**change from below**). These changes also involve different degrees of community awareness: changes from above normally involve processes of standardization or the importation of variants from outside the community, and are above the level of community awareness. In contrast, changes from below involve processes that speakers are not generally aware of until the change has progressed quite far. Speaker sex or gender is also implicated in patterns of language change. Although women tend to make more use of standard variants than do men, they also tend to adopt changes before men do. The apparent tendency of women to be both conservative and innovative (what Labov calls "the gender paradox") can be resolved by distinguishing between scenarios of variation: women are more conservative (standard) in situations of stable variation and are more innovative in changes in progress. Ethnicity has also been found to be an important consideration in language change, in that different ethnic groups may participate in or resist ongoing changes to different degrees. These social factors are all interactive, in that some cases may involve complex patterns of behaviour according to speaker sex, social class and ethnicity, which makes it important to understand the social context in which the change takes place.

7.1.2 Changes in Progress in Canadian English

Lexical Change

As noted above, the lexicon is the part of the linguistic system that is most susceptible to change, even across the lifespan of the individual speaker. Nevertheless, vocabulary also serves to mark different varieties of English. One of

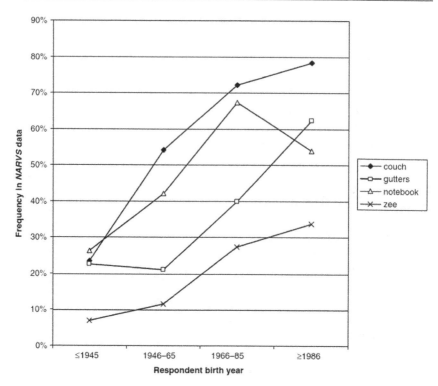

FIGURE 7.1 Distribution of American lexical variants in Canadian English by birth year
Source: Figure 4.3, Boberg 2010: 193.

the concerns in studies of Canadian English is the extent to which younger people are moving away from traditional Canadianisms in the lexicon toward greater use of Americanisms. Using the construct of apparent time, we can examine the distribution of Americanisms across age groups to infer ongoing changes in the Canadian English lexicon. Figure 7.1 shows the distribution of four Americanisms in Charles Boberg's NARVS data: *couch* (for Canadian *chesterfield*), *gutters* (for *eavestroughs*), *notebook* (for *scribbler*) and *zee* (for *zed*). Respondents are divided into four groups depending on their birth year: in or before 1945, between 1945 and 1965, between 1966 and 1985, and in or after 1986. For all four lexical variants, there is a steady increase in frequency the later the birth year of the respondent. The pattern in Figure 7.1 would seem to confirm the perception of the increasing Americanization of the Canadian English lexicon.

However, as noted above, the lexicon is a part of the linguistic system that is amenable to change across the lifespan. Rather than representing ongoing change in the Canadian English lexicon, the pattern in Figure 7.1 may in fact reflect age-grading, differences in vocabulary as a result of the

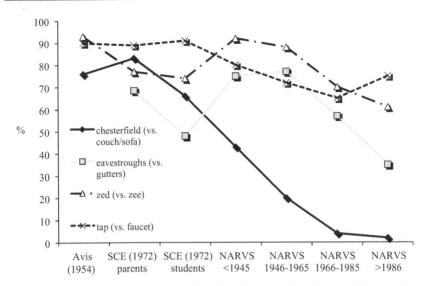

FIGURE 7.2 Distribution of Canadian lexical variants in Canadian English, in real and apparent time

Source: Adapted from Table 4.9, Boberg 2010: 194.

life-stage of the respondents. In order to decide between these two conclusions, we would need real-time data. Fortunately, some real-time data is available, in the form of dialect surveys conducted at earlier points in time. Figure 7.2 shows Boberg's (2010) combination of the results of NARVS with those of two earlier studies. In the 1950s, Walter Avis conducted a survey of Ontario examining differences between Canadian and American speech (Avis 1954). The *Survey of Canadian English* (SCE; Scargill and Warkentyne 1972) was conducted around 1970 and contained its own apparent-time division of ninth-grade students (who would have been born in the late 1950s) and their parents (who would have been born in the 1930s). Although the different surveys did not examine exactly the same communities or variants, taken together they offer an approximation of real-time data in order to answer questions about Americanization. Figure 7.2 charts the distribution of four Canadianisms: *chesterfield* (for *couch* or *sofa*), *eavestroughs* (for *gutters*), *zed* (for *zee*) and *tap* (for *faucet*). The pattern in Figure 7.2 offers a slightly more nuanced picture of the status of Canadianisms in Figure 7.1. The lexical variant *chesterfield* has clearly undergone a substantial decrease in both real and apparent time (to the extent that respondents born in or after 1986 almost never use it), and the other three Canadian variants have undergone a gradual decrease, but they are still the preferred variant for most of the respondents in NARVS, even those in the youngest age group. These results suggest that, although there may be an increasing Americanization of Canadian English vocabulary, it is not proceeding at the same rate for all lexical variables, and (with some exceptions) any change is very gradual.

Phonetic and Phonological Change

As with lexical variables, phonetic and phonological variables often serve to mark social and national identity. Also, as noted above, differences among varieties of English are marked primarily by differences in accent, especially in the realm of vowels, where mergers, splits and shifts have served to differentiate the vowel systems of English varieties since their spread around the world. Because there do not seem to be any changes occurring in the consonant system of Canadian English, in this section I focus on the most salient change occurring in the vowel system, the Canadian Vowel Shift (CVS).

As discussed in Chapter 5, the CVS primarily involves the lowering and retraction of the front lax vowels /ɪ/, /ɛ/ and /æ/, which Clarke et al. (1995) argue to have been triggered by the merger of /ɑ/ and /ɔ/. If the CVS is an ongoing change, we expect to see this reflected in the distribution of the realization of these vowels by age, with younger speakers featuring more lowered and retracted realizations. Figure 7.3, taken from Boberg (2010), plots the F1 and F2 values for a number of key vowel variables for speakers from three major Canadian cities (Vancouver, Montreal and Halifax), with speakers divided into two age groups: those born in or before 1965 and those born after 1965. As Figure 7.3 shows, younger speakers have visibly lowered and somewhat more retracted realizations for the front lax vowels than do older speakers (a difference that Boberg finds to be statistically significant).

However, because the vowel measurements combine speakers from different parts of the country, where the shift may be proceeding at different rates (and in qualitatively different ways), it would be more revealing to examine the progress of the shift among speakers of different ages in one location. Figure 7.4 presents the results of a study conducted in Toronto by Becky Roeder and Lidia Jarmasz (2010) in which speakers were divided not only by age group (22–53 years old and 72–85 years old) but also by speaker sex. As Figure 7.4 shows, differences among groups for /ɪ/ are not significantly different (although there is a slight tendency for younger speakers to have a more shifted realization of this vowel). However, both /ɛ/ and /æ/ exhibit the same pattern: younger speakers of both sexes have much more lowered and retracted realizations of these vowels than do older speakers, and within each age group women have more shifted realizations than do men. In other words, not only do we see a distribution for two components of this shift in apparent time, but the patterning for sex is consistent with change in progress, with women leading.

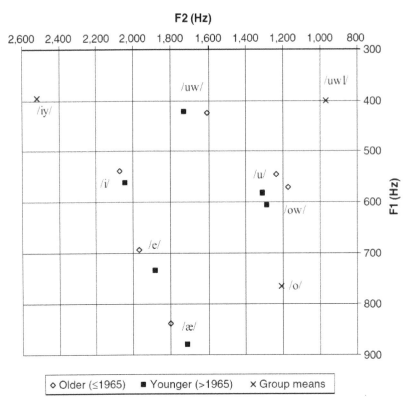

FIGURE 7.3 Acoustic measurements of Canadian English vowels (in Vancouver, Montreal and Halifax) for two age groups

Source: Figure 5.3, Boberg 2010: 230.

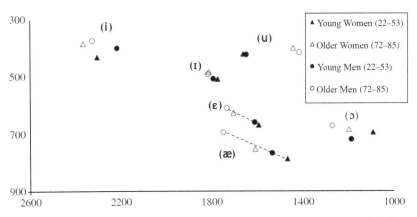

FIGURE 7.4 Normalized means for six vowels for 33 speakers of Toronto English, by sex and age group

Source: Adapted from Figure 2, Roeder and Jarmasz 2010: 393.

Grammatical Change

As we saw in Chapter 6, grammatical features do not generally serve to distinguish among varieties of English, and Canadian English is not characterized by salient grammatical variation (except for some regional varieties such as Newfoundland and Labrador English). However, we also saw that a consideration of the patterning of grammatical variables involves not only the presence or absence of a variant, or even its overall rate, but also the conditioning of that feature by language-internal factors. Nevertheless, if there are grammatical changes occurring in Canadian English, we expect to see different distributions of features (and/or their conditioning) across time.

Sali Tagliamonte (2006a) has identified a number of grammatical and discourse features that are examples of ongoing change in Canadian English. Two of these are the uses of the verb *have* (*to*) discussed in Chapter 6, varying between *have* (*to*), *have got* (*to*) and *got* (*to*) in its functions of expressing possession (7.1) and deontic modality (7.2), where it competes with *must*. Expression of future time varies between a modal construction with *will* and the semi-modal *going to* (7.3). Predicate adjectives can be intensified with *very*, *really* or *so* (7.4). At the level of discourse-pragmatics, there is variation with sentence tags such as *so* and *whatever* and "general extenders" such as *and stuff* (7.5). (Examples from Tagliamonte 2006.)

(7.1) a. It *has* a huge diving platform, diving tower and an Olympic size pool and we'*ve got* hundreds of thousands of people going into that pool. (TOR/N/E)

      b. So you *have* a mixture of you-know, highly educated people, you *got* a lot of actors and professors, right? (TOR/N/.)

(7.2) a. Because like, now in all high schools, by law you *must* have a security guard. (TOR/2/p)

      b. And I *gotta* say, that's pretty lucky.

      c. I said "You *have to* come up." I said "You *must* come up." And um the person on the phone, I said "I'*ve gotta* go." (TOR/N/s)

(7.3) Music's *gonna* evolve and change, so language *will* evolve and change too. (TOR/I/1)

(7.4) a. If he's *really* dull, but he's like, *so* hot . . . (TOR/2/a)

      b. It was *very* pretty . . . I loved her hair, it was amazing . . . And it was *really* pretty. (TOR/2/m)

(7.5) a. It's about like animals and stuff, *right?* (TOR/2/e)

      b. He worked at Sears doing all sorts of weird and wonderful systems analysis *and stuff like that.* (TOR/I/_)

      c. They would sing for hours, *you know.* (TOR/I/9)

      d. It's just like herbal like Chinese stuff, *whatever.* (TOR/I/_)

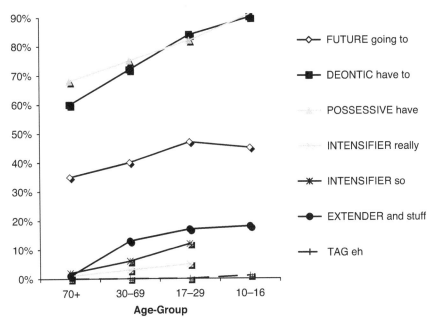

FIGURE 7.5 Ongoing grammatical changes in Canadian English

Source: Adapted from Tagliamonte 2006a.

Figure 7.5 shows the distribution of the incoming variants according to four age groups: teenagers (10–16), young adults (17–29), adults (30–69) and seniors. All of the variants show an increase in apparent time, though the strongest gains are made by *have (to)*.

Perhaps the most dramatic change in grammatical variation in Canadian English is the change in the system of quotative verbs. From a system that began with the use of *verba dicendi* such as *say* to constructions using the verb *go*, the system has overwhelmingly shifted to the use of *be like* (7.6). (Example from Tagliamonte 2006a.)

(7.6)   We*'re like*, "How was it?"
        And they*'re like*, "Oh, it was different."
        We*'re like*, "'Good' different?"
        They*'re like*, "You'll see, you'll see." (TOR/N/@)

Figure 7.6 shows the distribution of *be like* in comparison with other quotatives, based on data collected in 2004 (Tagliamonte and D'Arcy 2007). Older groups show little use of quotative *be like*—in fact, it only really takes off among the under-40 speakers. If the distribution according to age group can be interpreted as reflecting apparent time, this suggests that *be like* appeared as a quotative strategy beginning in the 1980s.

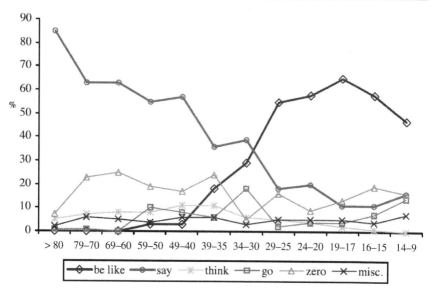

FIGURE 7.6 Overall distribution of quotative variants in Toronto English, by age group

Source: Figure 2, Tagliamonte and D'Arcy 2007: 205.

7.3 ETHNOLINGUISTIC VARIATION AND CHANGE

In Chapter 3, we noted a major change in patterns of immigration to Canada. The traditional sources of immigration, the United States and the British Isles, gave way in the 20th century to immigration from eastern and southern Europe. Beginning in the 1970s, primary immigration shifted to Asia, with the largest proportion of immigration from south Asia (India and Pakistan) and China. This shift in the sources of immigration has dramatically changed the ethnolinguistic profile of Canada's English-speaking population. Moreover, the tendency for more recent immigrants to settle in cities rather than in the countryside has enhanced the rural–urban split that developed in the 19th century. According to the 2011 census, while 21% of the population of Canada report being born outside of the country, this figure rises to 23% in Montreal, 40% in Vancouver and 46% in Toronto. I will focus on studies conducted on different ethnic groups in two of these cities.

Although the English-speaking community in Montreal has not been affected as much by recent changes in patterns of immigration, it has historically consisted of three ethnic groups: British/Irish, Italian and Jewish. If this social division is linguistically meaningful, we would expect to see it reflected in differences of patterning by the ethnic background of the speaker. Figure 7.7 shows Charles Boberg's (2010) plot of the F2 and F1 means for Montreal speakers, divided by ethnic background, while Table 7.2 shows the levels of significance for pairwise comparisons in differences in vowel measurements between ethnic groups. Note that the Italians

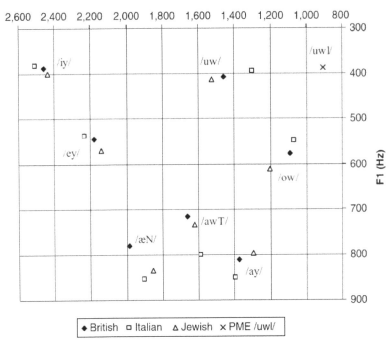

FIGURE 7.7 Mean values for selected vowels of Montreal English, by ethnic group (PME refers to the overall results for Boberg's *Phonetics of Montreal English* project)

Source: Figure 5.2, Boberg 2010: 222.

TABLE 7.2

Levels of Significance for Differences Between Vowel Measurements for Three Ethnic Groups in Montreal English (shading indicates differences that are not significant at the .05 level)

	Irish vs. Italian	Irish vs. Jewish	Italian vs. Jewish
F2 (u:)	.002	.896	.000
F1 (o:)	.914	.038	.047
F2 (o:)	.726	.002	.004
F1 (aw)	.003	.419	.068
F2 (aw)	.212	.546	.013
F2 (awN)	.033	.995	.017
F1 (ay)	.015	.853	.040
F2 (æN)	.026	.004	.559
F1 (ɒ)	.026	.838	.074
F2 (ɔ:)	.107	.803	.301

Source: Adapted from Table 7, Boberg 2004a: 556

have significantly less fronted /u/ and less raised /aw/ and /ay/ than the other groups. The Jewish informants are distinguished from the other groups in having significantly more fronted /o/, and the British/Irish have significantly more raised /æ/ before nasals. These results confirm that differences in ethnic background have consequences for the phonetic realization of Canadian English vowels.

The English-speaking community of Toronto is home to large numbers of people who speak a heritage language (HL) other than English. In the 2011 census, over 70 languages have at least 1,000 people who claim a HL as their mother tongue. Figure 7.8 shows the ethnic groups (other than British/Irish, French, Canadian and American) with most robust demographic representation in the city, along with the number of respondents claiming the associated HL as their mother tongue and home language.[1] The disparities between the number of people claiming a particular ethnic background and those claiming

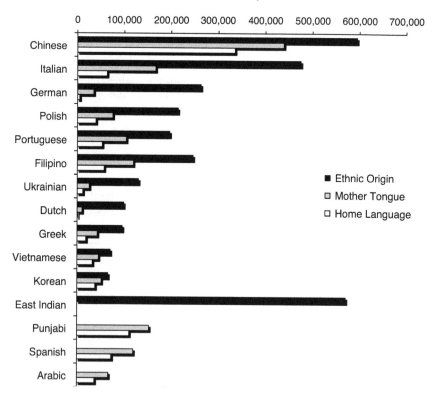

FIGURE 7.8 Largest groups in Toronto with nonofficial mother tongues and home languages and ethnic origins other than British/Irish, French, Canadian and American, by number of respondents

Source: Statistics Canada 2011.

an associated mother tongue indicate the degree to which different ethnolinguistic groups have undergone language shift to English, and the discrepan-
cies between the number of people claiming each language as a mother tongue
and as a home language are indicative of the degree to which each HL is being
maintained. One factor promoting HL maintenance is the tendency for people
of particular ethnolinguistic backgrounds to concentrate in particular neighbourhoods in the city. Such "ethnic enclaves" allow residents to live and work to
some degree in the HL, but they have also been argued to impede the acquisition
of mainstream Canadian English, especially for children growing up in those
neighbourhoods. Some fear that the result of such "voluntary segregation" and
limited exposure to old-line norms of Canadian English will lead to the development of "ethnolects", ethnically marked ways of speaking the language.

If the ethnic background of residents of Toronto and the extent to which
they interact with members of the same ethnolinguistic background has linguistic consequences, we expect to see these differences reflected in the distribution of linguistic variants. Rather than relying on the neighbourhood
in which informants grew up to differentiate among young people of different ethnic backgrounds, Michol Hoffman and I have made use of an "ethnic
orientation" (EO) questionnaire, which allows us to additionally categorize
speakers as "high EO" or "low EO" (Hoffman and Walker 2010). High EO
informants are oriented to more ethnically homogeneous social networks,
claim knowledge of the HL and engage in community activities, while low
EO informants have fewer or weaker ties to their ethnic group and have more
diverse social networks. If EO has linguistic consequences, we expect to see
differences in the distribution of linguistic variants not only across groups
with different ethnic backgrounds but also within each group on the basis of
EO status.

Figure 7.9 shows the overall rates for five phonetic variables in Toronto
English, according to the ethnic groups with the most robust representation
in the city (Chinese and Italian, along with an old-line British/Irish group),
further divided according to EO status. The five variables are:

- (ε)-shifting and (æ)-shifting: Two components of the CVS, coded
  impressionistically.
- (TD): Deletion of word-final [t] and [d] in consonant clusters (as in *sand* ~
  san', *west* ~ *wes'*).
- (ING): Realization of word-final [ɪŋ] as [ɪn] ("dropping the *g*", as in *singing* ~ *singin'*).
- (NK): Stopping of word-final [ŋ] to [ŋk] or [ŋg].

The first two variables, as we have seen, represent a change in progress, and
the third and fourth variables represent stable variation. These variables were

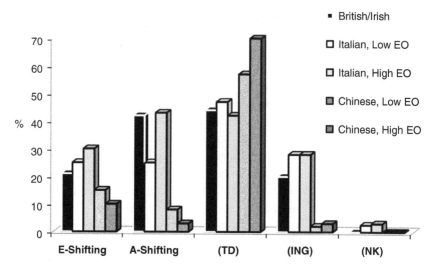

FIGURE 7.9 Overall rates of five phonetic variables in Toronto English, by ethnic background and ethnic orientation (EO)

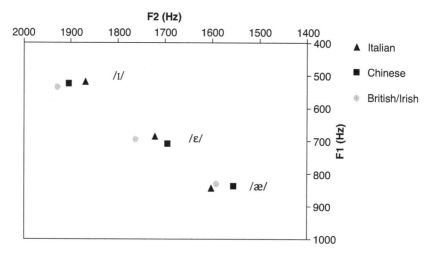

FIGURE 7.10 Mean vowel measurements for three components of the Canadian Vowel Shift, by ethnic group

Source: Hoffman 2010.

selected because they are likely to occur across all ethnic groups. The final variable represents a stereotypical feature of Italian Canadian English.

As Figure 7.10 shows, there are differences in ethnic background for all variables and, in some cases, differences in EO status. The Chinese, especially those of high EO status, lag in both components of the CVS and have significantly higher rates of (TD) and low rates of (ING). The Italians match or even outperform the British/Irish in the CVS, have the highest rate of (ING) and, as expected, are the only group to exhibit (NK) (albeit at very low rates). These results indicate clearly that the social divisions in ethnic background and, to some extent, in EO status have linguistic consequences. But do they also indicate the fragmentation of Canadian English in its largest city into different ethnolects? We can answer this question by looking not only at the overall rates of use but also the conditioning of the variation by language-internal factors. Regardless of overall rates of use, if speakers of different ethnic backgrounds exhibit the same linguistic conditioning of the variation, they can be taken to have the same underlying linguistic system.

The results for the two components of the CVS shown in Figure 7.9 were coded impressionistically on the basis of how frequently the coders heard speakers producing shifted vowels. Figure 7.10 shows an acoustic measurement of the same speakers, with F1 and F2 means plotted for three components of the shift (/ɪ/, /ɛ/ and /æ/) for the three ethnic groups (Hoffman 2010). Clearly the ethnic groups are not differentiated by the phonetic realization of any component of the shift, and pairwise comparison shows these differences not to be significant. Figures 7.11 and 7.12 show the language-internal

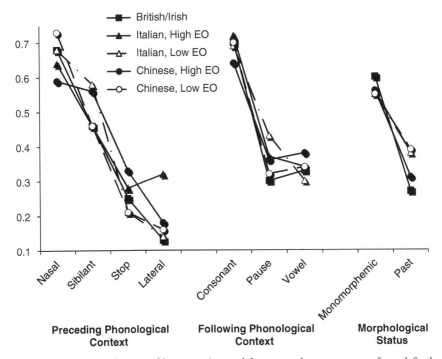

FIGURE 7.11 Contribution of language-internal factors to the occurrence of word-final (t/d)-deletion in Toronto English, by ethnic background and ethnic orientation (EO) status (factor weights)

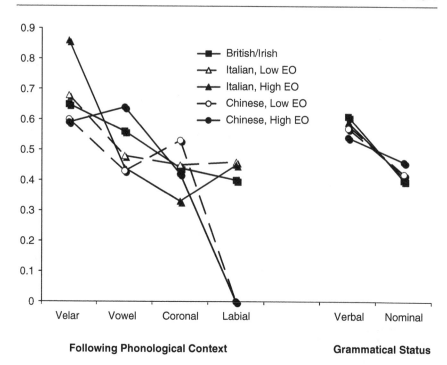

FIGURE 7.12 Contribution of language-internal factors to the occurrence of word-final *-in'* in Toronto English, by ethnic background and ethnic orientation (EO) status (factor weights)

conditioning of (TD) and (ING) for the speakers in Figure 7.9, with the values representing factor weights ranging from 0 to 1: the preceding and following phonological context and the grammatical status of each variable, marking past tense or not for (TD) and nominal or verbal for (ING). With a couple of exceptions (where the number of tokens for a category is small), the results are parallel regardless of ethnic background or EO status, suggesting that, regardless of the overall rates of occurrence, all the speakers analyzed here share the same underlying system of Canadian English. These results argue against predictions that Canadian English is undergoing ethnic fragmentation in the largest cities.

SUMMARY

This final chapter examined ways in which variation in the linguistic features of Canadian English is conditioned by social factors rather than by region or by language-internal considerations.

We began by considering the relationship between language variation and change, and how recognizing the fact of linguistic variation can help us to understand and explain language change. Identifying a number of questions that any study of language change must try to answer, we outlined the different methods for inferring change. In the absence of real-time data, the construct of apparent time allows us to infer change from distribution of variants by age-group, although we must be aware of the possibility of age-grading. Factors such as social class, sex and ethnicity may also help us to understand the social context of language change.

We considered a number of ongoing changes in Canadian English. There is evidence for Americanization of the Canadian lexicon, although it is not proceeding as quickly as some might believe. The Canadian Vowel Shift is an ongoing change in the vowel system of General Canadian English that appears to be proceeding across the entire country. Finally, the incursion of *be like* into the quotative system of Canadian English is a fairly rapid and recent change.

Perhaps the most salient aspect of Canada's largest cities is their increasing ethnolinguistic diversity, which has led some to argue that the nature of Canadian English is changing. Studies of different phonetic features in Montreal and Toronto do reveal differences among ethnic groups in the overall rate with which they use certain features and at which they participate in ongoing changes. However, if we focus not only on differences in overall rates but examine the linguistic conditioning of the variation, we find that the speakers of different ethnic backgrounds in Toronto show largely parallel conditioning. The results of this study suggest that all these speakers share the same underlying system of Canadian English and that fears about the loss of the distinctive nature of Canadian English are largely unfounded.

NOTE

1 The category "Chinese" is problematic because it includes a number of different national origins (Hong Kong, Taiwan, mainland China and so on) and languages/dialects. Cantonese is the specific Chinese language with the largest number of mother-tongue claimants. Similarly, the category "East Indian" is associated with a number of different national origins and languages. Punjabi is the South Asian language with the largest number of mother-tongue claimants. Spanish and Arabic are languages that are associated with multiple ethnic backgrounds.

Glossary

accomplishment A dynamic situation that has duration and an inherent end point.

achievement A dynamic situation that has an inherent end point but no duration.

acoustic phonetics The study of the production of human speech sounds that makes use of physical measurements of the sound wave.

activity A dynamic situation that has duration but no inherent end point.

affective The emotional or reactive component of language attitudes.

affixation A morphological process that involves the addition of an affix (e.g. a prefix or suffix) to a word stem.

age-grading The distribution of linguistic variation by age that reflects changes across the lifespan of the individual.

allomorph A variant form of a morpheme.

allophone A variant form of a phoneme.

alveolar A speech sound articulated at the alveoleum (the ridge behind the upper front teeth).

apparent time The use of the distribution of linguistic variation by age to infer language change in progress.

approximant A speech sound produced by slightly constricting the airflow.

articulatory phonetics The study of speech sounds that makes reference to the physiology of the vocal tract.

aspect A property of verbs and sentences that concerns the internal structure of situations and events.

aspiration A secondary articulation of consonants that involves an additional burst of airflow.

back (vowel) A vowel articulated further back in the mouth.

category (syntactic) The part of speech to which a word belongs (e.g. noun, verb).

central (vowel) A vowel articulated in the middle of the mouth.

chain shift A reorganization of the vowel system in which each vowel moves into the space formerly occupied by its neighbouring vowel.

change from above A language change initiated by higher social classes, usually above the level of speaker awareness.

change from below A language change initiated by lower social classes, usually below the level of speaker awareness.

cognitive The knowledge or set of beliefs that informs language attitudes.

communal change A pattern of language change in which individuals change in the same direction as the community.

complementary distribution A distribution of variant forms such that the contexts in which they occur do not overlap.

complementizer A function word that introduces a subordinate clause (e.g. *that*).

componential analysis Analysis of anthropological events or concepts that involves breaking them down into their constitutive parts.

compounding A process of word formation that involves combining two or more word roots.

conative The behavioral component of language attitudes.

consonant A speech sound produced by constricting the airflow.

constituent A unit of syntactic structure.

conventional implicature An utterance whose meaning is not directly reflected in linguistic structure but is inferred by common understanding.

conversion A morphological process that changes the meaning but not the form of the word.

coordination A syntactic construction that joins clauses through a conjunction such as *and* or *or*.

core linguistics The branches of linguistics concerned with language structure (phonetics, phonology, morphology, syntax).

derivation A morphological process that creates new lexemes.

descriptive linguistics A school of linguistics concerned with documenting language structure.

descriptivism An approach to language that involves describing linguistic structure and behavior without evaluating it as "good" or "bad".

diachronic linguistics An approach to the study of language that considers different points in time.

dialect area A geographical region defined by the co-occurrence of multiple isoglosses.

diphthong A speech sound involving two vowel articulations.

distinctive feature A property that defines a class of speech sounds.

egressive A speech sound produced by expelling air from the lungs.

ethnography of speaking An approach to sociolinguistics that makes use of the methods of anthropology.

etymology The history or origin of a word or the study of word histories or origins.

formant A concentration of energy in the sound wave that can be used to identify the configuration of the vocal tract.

fricative A consonant produced by holding the articulator close to the point of articulation.

front (vowel) A vowel articulated at the front of the mouth.

functional (category) A word that serves a grammatical function.

fundamental frequency The property of the sound wave that indicates pitch.

generative grammar A school of linguistics that views linguistic structure as generated by rules or principles.

glide A speech sound produced by slightly constricting the airflow.

glottal A speech sound articulated at the glottis.

grammaticalization A process by which a lexical category takes on functional properties.

head The syntactic category on which a phrase is based.

high (vowel) A vowel articulated toward the top of the mouth.

ideology A set of beliefs.

inflection A morphological process that does not create new lexemes.

ingressive A speech sound produced by inhaling air into the lungs.

intonation A suprasegmental property of the speech signal that concerns patterns of pitch.

isogloss A line on a map indicating the boundary between the geographical ranges of variant linguistic forms.

labial A speech sound articulated at the lips.

labiodental A speech sound articulated with the lips and front teeth.

lax (vowel) A vowel articulated lower in the mouth than its tense counterpart.

length A property of speech sounds concerned with their (relative) duration.

lexeme An entry in the mental lexicon that minimally includes all of the non-predictable properties of a word or morpheme.

lexical (category) A word that refers to something outside of language.

lexical borrowing A process by which words from one language are adopted into another language.

lexical semantics The branch of semantics that is concerned with the meaning of words.

lexicography The writing and production of dictionaries.

linguistic anthropology A branch of sociolinguistics that makes use of the methods of anthropology, or a branch of anthropology that is concerned with the linguistic aspects of culture.

linguistics The study of language.

low (vowel) A vowel articulated toward the bottom of the mouth.

manner of articulation The degree of constriction with which a speech sound is produced.

matched-guise test A method of studying language attitudes that involves playing recordings of the same speaker in different guises (accents or languages) and having listeners evaluate the recordings for social or personal characteristics.

mental lexicon The storage of sound-meaning correspondences in the speaker's brain.

merger A sound change in which two phonemes become one.

monomorphemic A word consisting of a single morpheme.

morpheme The minimal unit of linguistic structure that links sound and meaning.

morphology The branch of linguistics concerned with word structure.

narrative A sequentially ordered series of events that happened once, recounted by the speaker.

nasal A speech sound produced by passing air through the nasal cavity.

nasalization A secondary articulation of vowels in which air is passed through the nasal cavity.

neologism The creation of a new lexeme.

North Americanism A word that only occurs in North American English (Canadian or American) or has a preferred distribution or unique meaning there.

orthography A system of writing or spelling.

palatal A consonant articulated at the hard palate.

palato-alveolar A consonant articulated between the alveolum and the hard palate.

panel study A study of language change that samples the same speakers at different points in time.

philology The study of dead languages.

phonation The method with which a speech sound is produced, primarily with reference to the vocal cords.

phoneme A sound that serves to contrast meaning within a language.

phonetics The study of speech production.

phonology The study of sound patterns in language.

phrase A syntactic unit consisting of a category and its complement(s) and adjunct(s).

phrase-structure rule A statement of the possible ordering of phrases and of syntactic categories within phrases in a language.

place of articulation The point in the vocal tract at which a sound is produced.

plosive A consonant articulated through complete closure of the vocal tract.

pragmatics The study of meaning above the level of the sentence or proposition; the use of language in conversational interaction.

predicate The part of a sentence that describes the subject.

prescriptivism The belief that there are right and wrong forms of language.

propositional semantics An approach to the study of meaning that considers the meaning of the entire sentence.

psycholinguistics The branch of linguistics that considers the psychological aspects of language.

real time A longitudinal study of language change.

regionalism A word that only occurs within a particular region or has a preferred distribution or unique meaning there.

rhotic A speech sound with *r* quality, or a variety of language in which postvocalic *r* is pronounced.

root A morphological unit, the base upon which the word is built up.

rounded (vowel) A vowel sound produced with rounding of the lips.

secondary articulation A modification to the articulation of a speech sound.

segment A unit of phonetic articulation.

semantics The branch of linguistics concerned with meaning.

sociolinguistic interview A method of data collection used in sociolinguistics, in which informants are recorded speaking spontaneously on topics intended to focus more on what they are saying than how they are saying it.

sociolinguistics the branch of linguistics concerned with the social aspects of language.

sociolinguistic variation and change An approach to sociolinguistics that considers quantitative variation in language form and its conditioning by the linguistic and social context.

sociology of language The branch of sociolinguistics that considers large-scale patterns of language use.

sonorant A speech sound that normally occurs as voiced.

sound wave The physical realization of speech as bursts of energy.

spectrogram A visual representation of the concentrations of frequency in a sound wave.

speech act An utterance that fulfills a conversational function.

speech event A socially or culturally defined event that involves language.

state A nondynamic situation with duration but no inherent end point.

stem A unit of morphological structure, the base on which morphological processes act to create new words.

stem change A morphological process in which the sounds of the stem are modified.

stop A consonant articulated through complete closure of the vocal tract.

stress The relative prominence of a syllable within a word or phrase.

subject The part of a sentence that is described by the predicate.

subordinate clause A clause that acts as the object of a verb.

subordination Joining together clauses by making one clause the object of another.

suprasegmental A property of speech production beyond consonants and vowels, concerned with considerations of rhythm, stress and prosody.

synchronic linguistics An approach to linguistics that considers a language at only one point in time.

syntax The branch of linguistics concerned with word order.

tense A morphological property of verbs indicating time.

tense (vowel) A vowel articulated higher than its lax counterpart.

thematic role The semantic role of a noun phrase in the composition of the sentence.

trend study A study in real time that involves resampling the same community at different points in time.

velar A speech sound articulated at the velum (the soft palate).

vocal tract The physiological path from the glottis to the lips used to produce speech sounds.

voiced A speech sound articulated with vibration of the vocal cords.

voiceless A speech sound articulated without vibration of the vocal cords.

vowel A speech sound articulated without any constriction of airflow.

waveform A graphic representation of the sound wave.

word The smallest freestanding linguistic structure.

word list A list of words used to elicit phonetic forms in specific contexts.

Appendix: International Phonetic Alphabet

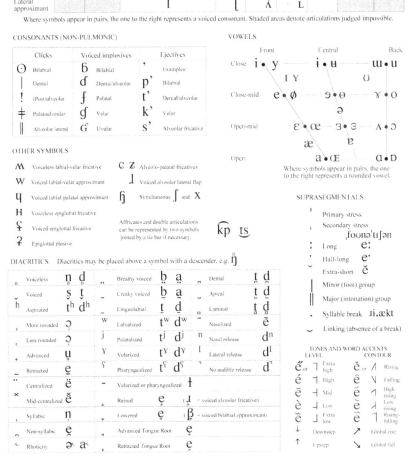

References

Avis, Walter S. 1954. Speech differences along the Ontario-United States border. I: Vocabulary. *Journal of the Canadian Linguistic Association* 1(1): 13–18.

Avis, Walter S. (ed.). 1962. *A Dictionary of Canadian English.* Toronto: W.J. Gage Ltd.

Avis, Walter S. (ed.). 1967. *A Dictionary of Canadianisms on Historical Principles.* Toronto: W.J. Gage Ltd.

Avis, Walter S. 1972. So *eh?* Is Canadian, eh? *Canadian Journal of Linguistics* 17: 89–104.

Barber, Katherine (ed.). 1998. *The Canadian Oxford Dictionary.* Don Mills, ON: Oxford University Press.

Bloomfield, Leonard. 1933. *Language.* New York: Henry Holt. Reprinted [1984] Chicago: University of Chicago Press.

Bloomfield, Morton W. 1948/1975. Canadian English and its relation to eighteenth century American speech. *Journal of English and Germanic Philology* 47: 59–66. [Reprinted in J.K. Chambers (ed.), *Canadian English: Origins and Structures.* Toronto: Methuen, 3–11.]

Boberg, Charles. 2004a. Ethnic patterns in the phonetics of Montreal English. *Journal of Sociolinguistics* 8(4): 538–68.

Boberg, Charles. 2004b. Canadian English. In Bernd Kortmann & Edgar W. Schneider (eds.), *A Handbook of Varieties of English: The Americas and the Caribbean.* Berlin: Mouton de Gruyter, 351–65.

Boberg, Charles. 2005. The North American Regional Vocabulary Survey: New variables and methods in the study of North American English. *American Speech* 80: 22–60.

Boberg, Charles. 2008. Regional phonetic differentiation in Standard Canadian English. *Journal of English Linguistics* 36(2): 129–54.

Boberg, Charles. 2010. *The English Language in Canada.* Cambridge: Cambridge University Press.

Boersma, Paul & David Weenink. 2015. Praat: Doing Phonetics by Computer [Computer program]. (http://www.praat.org).

Bordewich, Fergus M. 2005. *Bound for Canaan: The Underground Railroad and the War for the Soul of America.* New York: Harper Collins.

Brown, Thomas K. & Henry Alexander. 1937. *The Winston Simplified Dictionary for Canadian Schools.* Toronto: Winston.

Brunger, Alan G. 1990. The distribution of Scots and Irish in Upper Canada, 1851–71. *The Canadian Geographer/Le Géographe Canadien* 34(3): 250–58.

Bybee, Joan, Revere Perkins & William Pagliuca. 1993. *The Evolution of Grammar: Tense, Aspect and Modality in the Languages of the World.* Chicago: University of Chicago Press.

Cawdrey, Robert. 1604. *A Table Alphabeticall, Contayning and Teaching the True Writing and Vnderstanding of Hard Vsuall English Words, Borrowed from the Hebrew, Greeke, Latine, or French, &c.* London.

Cedergren, Henrietta. 1973. *Interplay of Social and Linguistic Factors in Panama.* Unpublished Ph.D. Dissertation, Cornell University.

Chambers, J.K. 1973/1975. Canadian Raising. *Canadian Journal of Linguistics* 18: 113–35. [Reprinted in J.K. Chambers (ed.), *Canadian English: Origins and Structures.* Toronto: Methuen, 83–100.]

Chambers, J.K. 1991. Canada. In Jenny Cheshire (ed.), *English Around the World: Sociolinguistic Perspectives.* Cambridge: Cambridge University Press, 89–107.

Chambers, J.K. 1993. "Lawless and vulgar innovations": Victorian views of Canadian English. In Sandra Clarke (ed.), *Focus on Canada.* Amsterdam: John Benjamins, 1–26.

Chambers, J.K. 1998a. Inferring dialect from a postal questionnaire. *Journal of English Linguistics* 26: 222–46.

Chambers, J.K. 1998b. English: Canadian varieties. In John Edwards (ed.), *Language in Canada.* Cambridge: Cambridge University Press, 252–72.

Chambers, J.K. 2000. Region and language variation. *English World-Wide* 21(2): 169–99.

Chambers, J.K. 2004. Dynamic typology and vernacular universals. In Bernd Kortmann (ed.), *Dialectology Meets Typology: Dialect Grammar from a Cross-Linguistic Perspective.* Berlin: Mouton de Gruyter, 127–45.

Chambers, J.K. 2007. Geolinguistic patterns in a vast speech community. *Linguistica Atlantica* 28: 27–36.

Clarke, Sandra. 2010a. Newfoundland and Labrador English. In Daniel Schreier, Peter Trudgill, Edgar W. Schneider & Jeffrey P. Williams (eds.), *The Lesser-Known Varieties of English: An Introduction.* Cambridge: Cambridge University Press, 72–91.

Clarke, Sandra. 2010b. *Newfoundland and Labrador English.* Edinburgh: Edinburgh University Press.

Clarke, Sandra, Ford Elms & Amani Youssef. 1995. The third dialect of English: some Canadian evidence. *Language Variation and Change* 7: 209–28.

Cowan, Helen I. 1961. *British Emigration to British North America: The First Hundred Years.* Revised and enlarged edition. Toronto: University of Toronto Press.

Cowan, Helen I. 1968. *British Immigration before Confederation.* Ottawa: The Canadian Historical Association Booklets.

Craig, Gerald. 1963. *Upper Canada: The Formative Years, 1784–1841.* Toronto: McClelland & Steward Ltd.

Crystal, David. 2004. *The Language Revolution.* Cambridge: Polity Press.

Dollinger, Stefan. 2008. *New-Dialect Formation in Canada: Evidence from the English Modal Auxiliaries.* Amsterdam/New York: John Benjamins.

Fishman, Joshua. 1968. *Readings in the Sociology of Language.* The Hague/Paris: Mouton.

Gold, Elaine & Mireille Tremblay. 2006. Eh? and Hein?: Discourse particles or national icons? *Canadian Journal of Linguistics* 51(2-3): 247–63.

Gregg, Robert J. 1992. The survey of Vancouver English. *American Speech* 67(3): 250–67.

Gregg, R.J., Gaelan Dodds de Wolf, Margery Fee & Janice McAlpine (eds.). 2004. *The Survey of Vancouver English: A Sociolinguistic Study of Urban Canadian English.* Strathy Occasional Papers on Canadian English 5. Kingston, ON: Strathy Language Unit.

Hoffman, Michol F. 2010. The role of social factors in the Canadian Vowel Shift: Evidence from Toronto. *American Speech* 85(2): 121–40.

Hoffman, Michol F. & James A. Walker. 2010. Ethnolects and the city: Ethnic orientation and linguistic variation in Toronto English. *Language Variation and Change* 22(1): 37–67.

Hopper, Paul J. 1991. On some principles of grammaticalization. In Elizabeth Closs Traugott and Bernd Heine (eds.), *Approaches to Grammaticalization, Volume 1*. Amsterdam: John Benjamins, 17–36.

Hymes, Dell. 1962/1968. The ethnography of speaking. In Thomas Gladwin and William C. Sturtevant (eds.), *Anthropology and Human Behavior*. Washington, DC: Anthropological Society of Washington, 15–53. [Reprinted in Joshua Fishman (ed.), *Readings in the Sociology of Language*. The Hague/Paris: Mouton, 99–138.]

ITP Nelson. 1996. *ITP Nelson Canadian Dictionary of the English Language*. Scarborough, ON: ITP Nelson.

Jasanoff, Maya. 2011. *Liberty's Exiles: American Loyalists in the Revolutionary World*. New York: Knopf.

Johnson, Daniel E. 2009. Getting off the GoldVarb standard: Introducing Rbrul for mixed-effects variable rule analysis. *Language and Linguistics Compass* 3(1): 359–83.

Johnson, Samuel. 1755. *A Dictionary of the English Language*. London: Printed by W. Strahan, for J. and P. Knapton; T. and T. Longman; C. Hitch and L. Hawes; A. Millar; and R. and J. Dodsley.

Joos, Martin. 1942/1975. A phonological dilemma in Canadian English. *Language* 18: 141–44. [Reprinted in J.K. Chambers (ed.), *Canadian English: Origins and Structures*. Toronto: Methuen, 79–82.]

Kachru, Braj B. 1992. *The Other Tongue: English across Cultures*. Champaign, IL: University of Illinois Press.

Kelley, Ninette & Michael Trebilcock. 1998. *The Making of the Mosaic: A History of Canadian Immigration Policy*. Toronto: University of Toronto Press.

Kiefte, Michael & Elizabeth Kay-Raining Bird. 2010. Canadian Maritime English. In Daniel Schreier, Peter Trudgill, Edgar W. Schneider & Jeffrey P. Williams (eds.), *The Lesser-Known Varieties of English: An Introduction*. Cambridge: Cambridge University Press, 59–71.

Knowles, Norman. 1997. *Inventing the Loyalists: The Ontario Loyalist Tradition and the Creation of Usable Pasts*. Toronto: University of Toronto Press.

Labov, William. 1963. The social motivation of a sound change. *Word* 19: 273–307.

Labov, William. 1966. *The Social Stratification of English in New York City*. Washington, DC: Center for Applied Linguistics.

Labov, William. 1984. Field methods of the Project on Linguistic Change and Variation. In John Baugh & Joel Sherzer (eds.), *Language in Use*. Englewood Cliffs, NJ: Prentice-Hall, 28–53.

Labov, William. 1989. The child as linguistic historian. *Language Variation and Change* 1: 85–97.

Labov, William. 1991. The three dialects of English. In Penelope Eckert (ed.), *New Ways of Analyzing Sound Change*. New York: Academic Press, 1–44.

Labov, William. 2007. Transmission and diffusion. *Language* 83(2): 344–87.

Labov, William, Sharon Ash & Charles Boberg. 2006. *The Atlas of North American English: Phonetics, Phonology and Sound Change*. Berlin: de Gruyter Mouton.

Labov, William, Paul Cohen, Clarence Robins & John Lewis. 1968. *A Study of the Nonstandard English of Negro and Puerto Rican Speakers in New York City*. United States Office of Education Final Report, Research Project No. 3288.

Landon, Fred. 1967. *Western Ontario and the American Frontier*. Toronto: McClelland and Stewart.

Lass, Roger. 1990. Where do extraterritorial Englishes come from? Dialect input and recodification in transported Englishes. In Sylvia M. Adamson, Vivien A. Law, Nigel Vincent & Susan Wright (eds.), *Papers from the 5th International Conference on English Historical Linguistics 1987*. Amsterdam: John Benjamins, 245–80.

Le Page, Robert & Andrée Tabouret-Keller. 1985. *Acts of Identity: Creole-Based Approaches to Language and Ethnicity*. Cambridge: Cambridge University Press.

Li, Peter S. 1998. *The Chinese in Canada*. Second edition. Toronto: Oxford University Press.

McDougall, Duncan. 1961. Immigration into Canada, 1851–1920. *Canadian Journal of Economics and Political Science* 27(2): 162–75.

Mika, Nick & Helma Mika. 1976. *United Empire Loyalists: Pioneers of Upper Canada*. Belleville, ON: Mika Publishing Company.

Milroy, James & Lesley Milroy. 1978. Belfast: Change and variation in an urban vernacular. In Peter Trudgill (ed.), *Sociolinguistic Patterns in British English*. London: Arnold, 19–36.

Mufwene, Salikoko. 2001. *The Ecology of Language Evolution*. Cambridge: Cambridge University Press.

Mufwene, Salikoko. 2008. *Language Evolution: Contact, Competition, and Change*. London: Continuum Press.

Orkin, Mark M. 1970. *Speaking Canadian English: An Informal Account of the English Language in Canada*. Toronto: General Publishing Company.

Poplack, Shana & Sali Tagliamonte. 1991/1993. African American English in the diaspora: The case of old-line Nova Scotians. *Language Variation and Change* 3(3): 301–39. [Reprinted in Sandra Clarke (ed.), *Focus on Canada*. Amsterdam: John Benjamins, 109–50.]

Poplack, Shana & Sali Tagliamonte. 2001. African Americans in Nova Scotia: Settlement and data. In *African American English in the Diaspora*. Oxford: Blackwell, 39–68.

Pratt, T. K. 1988. *Dictionary of Prince Edward Island English*. Toronto: University of Toronto Press.

Roeder, Rebecca & Lidia-Gabriela Jarmasz. 2010. *The Canadian Shift in Toronto. Canadian Journal of Linguistics/Revue canadienne de linguistique* 55(3): 387–404.

Sandilands, John. 1912. *Western Canadian Dictionary and Phrase-Book: Things a Newcomer Wants to Know*. Winnipeg: Telegram Job Printers Ltd.

Sankoff, David, Sali Tagliamonte & Eric Smith. 2012. GoldVarb Lion: A multivariate analysis application for Macintosh. (http://individual.utoronto.ca/tagliamonte/goldvarb.html).

Sankoff, Gillian & Hélène Blondeau. 2007. Language change across the lifespan: /r/ in Montreal French. *Language* 83(3): 560–88.

Sankoff, Gillian & Henrietta Cedergren. 1972. Sociolinguistic research on French in Montreal. *Language in Society* 1: 173–74.

Sapir, Edward. 1921. *Language: An Introduction to the Study of Speech*. New York: Harcourt.

Scargill, Matthew H. 1957/1975. The sources of Canadian English. *Journal of English and Germanic Philology* 56: 610–14. [Reprinted in J. K. Chambers (ed.), *Canadian English: Origins and Structures*. Toronto: Methuen, 12–15.]

Scargill, Matthew Henry & Henry J. Warkentyne. 1972. The Survey of Canadian English: A report. *English Quarterly* 5(3): 47–104.

Schneider, Edgar W. 2007. *Postcolonial English: Varieties around the World*. Cambridge: Cambridge University Press.

Statistics Canada. 2011. *Census Canada*. http://www.statcan.gc.ca

Story, George M., William J. Kirwin & John D. A. Widdowson (eds.). 1982. *Dictionary of Newfoundland English*. Toronto: University of Toronto Press.

Tagliamonte, Sali. 2006a. "So cool, right?": Canadian English entering the 21st century. *Canadian Journal of Linguistics* 51(2-3): 309–31.

Tagliamonte, Sali. 2006b. *Analysing Sociolinguistic Variation*. Cambridge: Cambridge University Press.

Tagliamonte, Sali & Alexandra D'Arcy. 2004. He's like, she's like: The quotative system in Canadian youth. *Journal of Sociolinguistics* 8: 493–514.

Tagliamonte, Sali & Alexandra D'Arcy. 2007. Frequency and variation in the community grammar: Tracking a new change through the generations. *Language Variation and Change* 19(2): 199–217.

Taylor, Alan. 2007. The Late Loyalists: Northern reflections of the early American republic. *Journal of the Early Republic* 27: 1–34.

Thibault, Pierrette & Michelle Daveluy. 1989. Quelques traces du passage du temps dans le parler des Montréalais, 1971–1984. *Language Variation and Change* 1: 19–45.

Thomas, Erik R. 1991. The origin of Canadian Raising in Ontario. *Canadian Journal of Linguistics/Revue canadienne de linguistique* 36: 147–70.

Trudgill, Peter. 1974. *The Social Differentiation of English in Norwich*. Cambridge: Cambridge University Press.

Trudgill, Peter. 1986. *Dialects in Contact*. Oxford: Blackwell.

Trudgill, Peter. 2000. *Sociolinguistics: An Introduction to Language and Society*. Fourth edition. London: Penguin.

Trudgill, Peter. 2004. *New-Dialect Formation: The Inevitability of Colonial Englishes*. Oxford: Oxford University Press.

Trudgill, Peter. 2006. Dialect mixture versus monogenesis in colonial varieties: The inevitability of Canadian English? *Canadian Journal of Linguistics* 51: 265–86.

Vincent, Diane, Marty Laforest & Guylaine Martel. 1995. Le corpus de Montréal 1995: Adaptation de la méthode d'enquête sociolinguistique pour l'analyse conversationnelle. *Dialangue* 6: 29–46.

Walker, James A. 2000. *Present Accounted For: Prosody and Aspect in Early African American English*. Unpublished Ph.D. Dissertation, University of Ottawa.

Walker, James A. 2007. "There's bears back there": Plural existentials and vernacular universals in (Quebec) English. *English World-Wide* 28(2): 147–66.

Walker, James W. St. G. 1993. *The Black Loyalists: The Search for a Promised Land in Nova Scotia and Sierra Leone, 1783–1870*. Toronto: University of Toronto Press.

Webster, Noah. 1828. *An American Dictionary of the English Language*. New York: S. Converse.

Weinreich, Uriel, William Labov & Marvin I. Herzog. 1968. Empirical foundations for a theory of language change. In Winfred P. Lehmann & Yakov Malkiel (eds.), *Directions for Historical Linguistics: A Symposium*. Austin: University of Texas Press, 95–188.

Wells, John C. 1982. *Accents of English, Volume 3: Beyond the British Isles*. Cambridge: Cambridge University Press, 490–97.

Winks, Robin W. 1997. *The Blacks in Canada: A History*. Montreal/Kingston: McGill-Queen's University Press.

Woods, Howard B. 1979. *A Socio-Dialectology Survey of the English Spoken in Ottawa: A Study of Sociological and Stylistic Variation in Canadian English*. Unpublished Ph.D. Dissertation, University of British Columbia.

Wynne, Graeme. 1987a. A province too much dependent on New England. *The Canadian Geographer* 31(20): 98–113.

Wynne, Graeme. 1987b. A region of scattered settlements and bounded possibilities: Northeastern America 1775–1800. *The Canadian Geographer* 31(4): 319–38.

Index

CPSIA information can be obtained
at www.ICGtesting.com
Printed in the USA
BVHW06s2039241018
531144BV00009B/207/P

9 780415 535373